W9-BJS-554

The Patchwork Mind

Trivia for Every Day of the Year

by

Guida Jackson

Houston, Texas

Cover design by Adam Murphy
Adapted from a glass mosaic by William H. Laufer

Manufactured in the United States of America
Published by Clarendon House

Printed and bound at
8888 Monroe Road
Houston, Texas

1 2 3 4 5 6 7 8 9 10

Library of Congress Cataloguing in Publication Data

Jackson, Guida M.
Patchwork mind, the, trivia for every day of the year

I. Memoirs II. Journals III. Mythology IV. Jungian psychology

V. Epics

ISBN 0-9771797-1-0

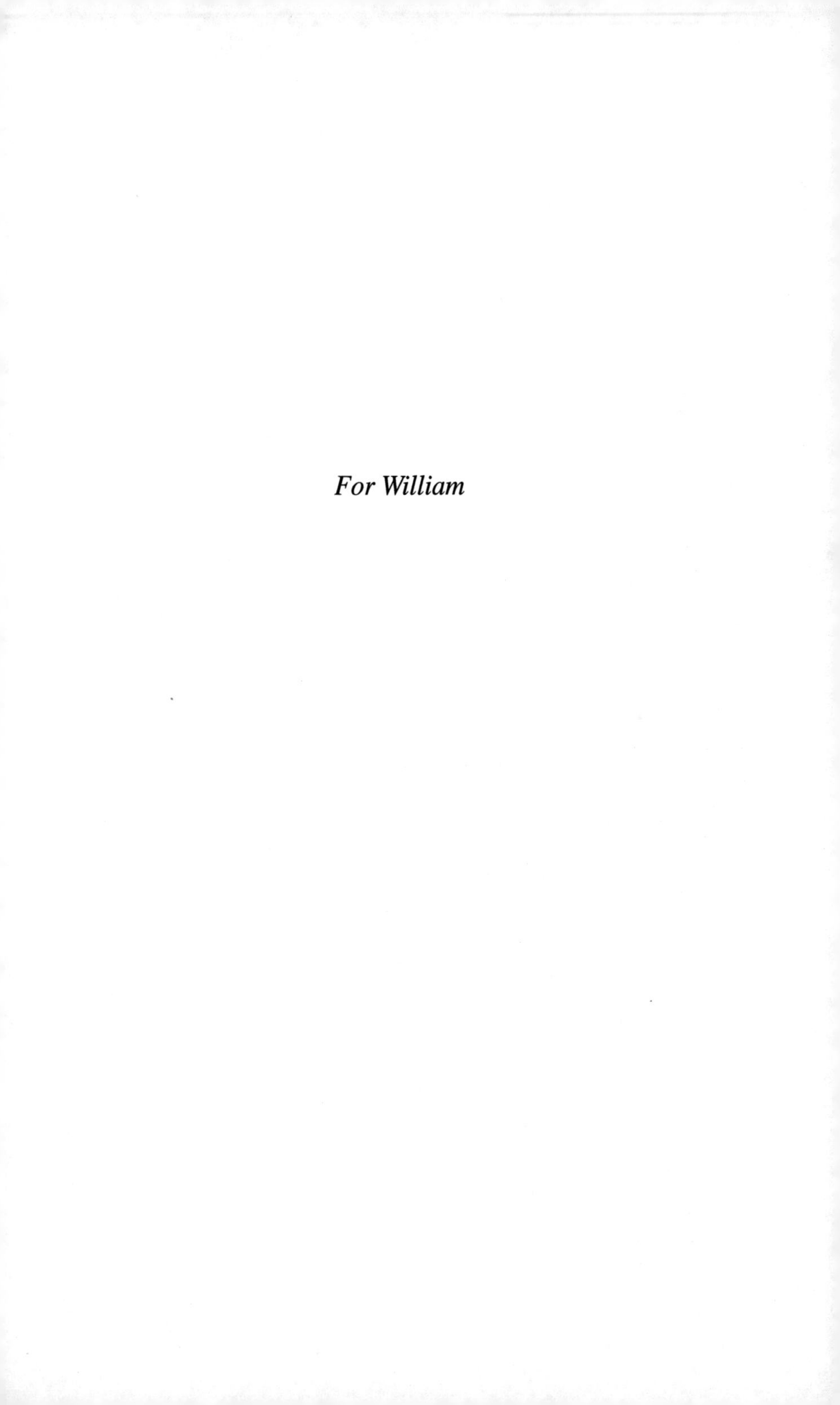

For William

Why this Book?

My late first husband, a doctor, often kidded that the reason I came up with trivia on various subjects was that my mind wasn't cluttered with important things. But he too picked up interesting trifles in the operating room and dispensed them over the family dinner table.

He remarked that colleagues who had done undergraduate studies in the humanities had a much broader range of knowledge than he, with his traditional pre-med BS degree. It was from generalists among his peers that he picked up his interesting trivia.

Once when something very unlikely happened that I had hoped would occur, he said, appearing awed, "You have an uncanny knack of making things turn out the way you want them to." This so impressed me (coming from a scientist!) that I immediately wrote it in my journal so I could ponder it later.

I've decided there's a kernel of truth in both his observations. My mind has never been filled with much science, which he considered the ruling element of our lives. I sometimes secretly doubted its conclusions and now have lived long enough to have an occasional suspicion vindicated, when science overturned itself. Even Stephen Hawking has announced that his previous hypothesis having to do with black holes was wrong.

As for the observation that I have a knack for making things turn out the way I want, well, sometimes we're lucky. Or maybe the knack is in wanting things the way they do turn out—and in seeing signs of which way the snow is drifting and deciding that's where I wanted it to be all along.

Anyway, even this man of science came to think that somehow I led a magical life, with my mind full of trivia. And my journals, one for every year, did overflow with a patchwork of trivia. I couldn't help being a generalist, making connections between things.

Our lives are punctuated by very few grand, momentous events. It is trivia, pieced around these events, that holds our days together. Trivia can be cherished as the rich stuff of a magical life.

It seemed a pity not share cullings from my journal, which make up my beliefs and, if you trust a man of science, my private magic.

Author's note: *I was blessed, as a child of eight, to fall heir to five books of Greek, Roman, Norse, German, and Celtic myth that had been adapted for children in the early part of the last century. This began a life-long love affair with the traditions of my ancestors.*

It was natural that my graduate work would be in the field of world literature. Dr. Michael Mahon of California State University, who directed my masters thesis and whose course on Archetypal Literary Criticism fired my imagination, urged me to continue the study. Dr. Abe Ravitz,who led my doctoral dissertation committee, directed me toward epics of Africa, India, Oceana, and the West, all of which bear a strong resemblance to their European counterparts.

In 1980, I signed up for a six-week study of symbols in literature with Veniece Standley at Analytical Psychology Studies, Inc. The project was so immense that I stayed for six years. I was introduced to authors, most Jungian psychologists, who analyze myth, legend, and tradition in literature as they affect our daily lives. Their insights and wisdom have informed my thinking ever since.

It became apparent early in my studies that we are much more like other cultures than we are different. We have built on the past, borrowing its traditions much as a church might be erected on the foundation of a temple belonging to an older culture. This was a comforting revelation, for it connected me with other worlds and grounded me in my shared ancient human heritage.

I am also indebted for this experience because the study of world myth was subsequently invaluable, not only in preparation of a college-level course which I taught on Archetype in Literature, but also in writing several books on the subject, notably The Encyclopedia of Traditional Epics, Encyclopedia of Literary Epics *(both ABC-CLIO) and* Traditional Epics, a Literary Companion *(Oxford University Press).*

Use of mythical characters as archetypes of behavioral traits has become part of my frame of reference. It will be helpful to the reader to keep that in mind while deciphering parts of this journal.

Contemplating Magic: January

January 1: * We have two periods of new beginnings in our Western calendar year: we celebrate both the new tradition and a more ancient one. The tradition of beginning a new year in January is actually scarcely 400 years old. Prior to that, for the Romans, New Year began on March 1. In ancient Babylon, Assyria, Phoenicia, Canaan and Israel, the celebration occurred on the new moon in the month of March, roughly coinciding with the vernal equinox. Among the Celts of Northern Europe, New Year's Day was November 1. Regardless of the date, the tradition, dating some 3500 years before the Christian era to ancient Sumeria, entails discarding the old to make way for the new. In Great Britain, Boxing Day, on the day after Christmas, owes its celebration to the Sumerians. Old things are boxed up and given to the less fortunate, making way in the household for the new. This entails refraining from looking back. Buddhists say: Look in the direction you want to go and start walking.

In some cultures, what happens on New Year's Day is a portent of what's to come. It is unlucky to carry over old business into the New Year, and unlucky for anything borrowed to remain in the house. That would presage being in debt all year.

In old Germany, New Year's Day is one of the Lostage, or oracle days, along with Christmas, Twelfth Night, and Midsummer. Pockets or cupboards should not be empty at this time. Breaking glass presages death, as does having a corpse in the house on New Year's Day. At daybreak, if the fire still burns, the year will prosper; if not, it will be a lean year. If a live ember rolls out, expect a death.

New Year's Day is a return to the first day of creation. It represents a reunion with the original conditions. In northern Europe, weather conditions on each of the twelve days of Christmas are omens of events in each of the twelve coming months.

* Isaiah 43:19: "I am about to do a new thing."

January 2: * Regardless of when we celebrate the New Year, something compels us to make resolutions. We might say that the resolution begins the magic because it is a *performative* statement. A *performative* sentence brings things into being, as in, "I take thee to be my wedded husband." Making a promise is a *performative* sentence. By stating your promise, you establish it as a commitment. We're familiar with the old magic word, "Abracadabra." One of the theories about its origin is that it comes from the Aramaic "abrakadibra" which means "Let it be created as it is spoken."

January 3: * Impeccable scholarly Torah researchers have found that the Genesis and Numbers authors have copied whole passages from Joshua and Judges and not the other way around.

* Will Durant: "The first lesson of philosophy is that we might all be wrong."

* *Vasana* is a Hindu Sanskrit word meaning, "perfumes," lingering consciousness of past perceptions: *deja vu*, in other words. Unconscious memories of past lives, the vasanas, predispose the transmigrating soul to act in one way or another in its new life.

January 4: * Here's a *miracle*: In its normal state, a slime mold colony consists of a large number of independent individuals, amoeba like cells that feed on vegetation on the forest floor. These cells multiply by simple division and spread out, eating everything in their path until there is no food left in the path of the colony. At this critical point, chemical signals move between the cells and trigger an entirely new form of behavior. The cells begin to congregate and become members of a single, multicellular animal that looks like a slug, which moves across the forest floor until it finds a suitable location. There, it rears up and develops a head on top of a long stalk. Within this head, spores form and shoot out in a sort of explosion. As each spore comes to rest, it produces an individual slime mold cell that begins it life of eating, dividing, and ultimately producing a new colony of cells.

British theoretical physicist F. David Peat, PhD, says, "As with the slime mold, so with the universe….Within each element of matter and space-time is enfolded the entire universe. The collective order that is contained within an individual mold cell can also be found in the world of ants, bees, wasps, and termites. While the single insect seems to be living an independent existence, it also carries within it…the behavior of the hive or the colony."

January 5: * Fruit flies, artificially genetically deprived of eyes for several generations, will develop eyes again. There is no biological explanation, except that, when the master plan has been altered, it will correct itself in time. This fits in with Sinnott's book on *The Biology of the Spirit.*

January 6: * This is Christian Epiphany, or Three Kings' Day, but according to the old Julian calendar, this is observed as Christmas. The island of Foula, 27 miles west of Scalloway in the Shetland Islands is one of the last places in Europe to continue to observe Christmas on this date. The rest of Scotland changed to December 25 in 1752, a date that had been decreed by the Roman emperor Constantine the Great in 325 A.D. The reason was that the date had been associated with other gods, most notably "the Son of God" and "the Light of the World" from pre-Christian times: It was the birth date of the Persian god Mithras, who was born on December 25, was buried in a rock tomb, and resurrected three days later. It was the birth date of the Egyptian god Osiris. It was the birth date of the Greek god Dionysus and possibly of Adonis, as well. I felt betrayed when I learned this. Much the way I felt when I was told by a friend, Margaret Ann Jenkins, that there is no Santa Claus.

January 7: * As a pre-television kid, I read everything I could find, including my mother's old college textbooks. One in particular fascinated me from about nine year on: *The Evolution of Animal Intelligence* by S. J. Holmes, PhD, of The U. of California.It was published in 1911 and had belonged to someone named Thelma Parker before my mother got it. There was a passage that I returned to year after year: "If we would avoid the assumption of an absolute beginning of consciousness, we may hold that something akin to consciousness, but very much more primitive than any of the forms of it with which we are acquainted, exists in connection with all inorganic processes." My mind grabbed onto this because it affirmed what I instinctively felt was true. I saw no conflict between what I read in this book and what I read in the Bible, which I also devoured from cover to cover in several translations, along with some old epic books that told myths of other cultures. I grew up with the understanding that the Bible was also made up of epics and that some of them at least were allegorical, meaning that they explained the inexplicable, the ineffable, with stories that we simple humans could understand. So I was cheered by this great truth which I found in Mother's old textbook. It was comforting to know how connected I was with the rest of creation.

Many years later, when I was about fifty, I told her about how many times I had read the book and about the passage that meant so much to me. I went to her bookshelf, pulled down the book, and it naturally fell open to the statement I quoted above. Mother was astonished and said, "You must take the book, then." I wrapped it in a plastic bread wrapper and brought it back to Houston, where it has a special place in my study, beside some seven or eight Bibles.

January 8: * I get a religious experience about mathematics. It appears to express timeless truth, valid everywhere and for all time. Numbers can work magic. The laws of mathematics of nature appear to be eternal and to have existed always, even before the cosmos began. They seem like ideas in a universal mind. Ancient Pythagoreanistism gave us the feeling that there is a kind of knowing which penetrates to the core of the universe, which offers truth as something both beatific and comforting, so that the human being feels cradled in a universal harmony. When an algebraic formula works its magic, I do feel this sense of both awe and safety.

I've noticed that people who are musical are often good at mathematics. It has something to do with brain organization. I keep thinking about those German geniuses who put together the huge complicated music-making machines. When you see their intricacies and listen to the enchanting music they produce, you feel you're in the presence of something divine. A nineteenth-century physicist, Heinrich Hertz, said, "One cannot escape the feeling that these mathematical formulae have an independent existence and an intelligence of their own, that they are wiser than we."

Recently I read about a Harvard physics professor, Lisa Randall, who looks younger than my daughter. With Raman Sundrum she has published two papers that have transformed the way physicists think about the underlying structure of space, by showing that the hidden dimensions required by string theory could be not just large but infinite, provided space was warped in the right way. Her thesis effectively solves the geometry of a high-dimensional model of space. Her papers are now among the most cited in particle physics. The most interesting statement to me in her interview was: "The theory predicts that for every particle we know about, there will be an additional particle."

On religion, she said, "All the work I've done makes me think the existence of God less likely. I want solutions and God just seems like such a cop-out."

Most of this young professor's findings are too deep for me. They all spring from her incredible scientific mind. But some things germinate in the heart. I keep thinking of the Chinese proverb: "Better to believe too much than nothing at all." I take solace in the striking spread of Pentecostal religions around the world, stressing as they do the immediacy of a transcendence presence. I still think there's something ineffable about mathematics. And so did Einstein.

January 9: * "Whatever thy hand finds to do, do it with all thy might." This biblical quote has been with me all my life. A former student professes to be a writer. Years go by and when we meet I ask, "Have you written anything yet?" She, being very religious, always answers, "I'm waiting for the Lord to tell me what to write."

There's another form of passivity: perfectionism. "If I can't be perfect, I won't do anything." I read in an interview with a man who won both a Pulitzer for cartooning and a Tony for playwriting: "My sister wanted to be the writer in the family, but she never wrote. Her sense of herself was so grandiose that she couldn't take on a basic prerequisite of being a writer, which is to get your head bashed in. If you have the illusion of your own untamperable excellence, it is hard to submit to anyone else's judgment. She could never do that."

The *Bhagavad-Gita* says we should do our work, do our duty the best we can, but not be attached to the outcome. This advice is spoken by the Hindu god Ardjuna (Arjuna) and the inference is, regardless of our puny efforts, the gods will make things turn out the way they're supposed to.

With our intent, we play a crucial part, and it's critical to focus on the goal and not get attached to a particular process for getting there. Yet, do ends justify the means? But if we're focused on the process rather than the destination, we may end up somewhere else.

Still, who knows but what the journey is the whole point, anyway.

January 10: * There is such a thing as a cultural move toward consciousness. This has been demonstrated by the popular example of the "hundredth money," where, soon after a monkey on a remote Pacific island learned to wash her sweet potatoes before eating, she taught her young to do the same, and before long, even monkeys on adjoining islands were washing their sweet potatoes as well. In England, back when milk was delivered to the door in glass bottles with paper caps, one tiny tit learned to peck its way through the top and drink the milk. Soon tits all over England were doing the same to milk bottles on thousands of doorsteps.

The phenomenon refers to humans, too. When one person is more conscious, it changes the consciousness of everyone in the room. Some groups become super-charged with creativity. The renewing of personal faith is a process inextricably bound up with the collective renewal of faith. In some deep way the individual opus has a healing effect on the collective as well.

Thoreau said something on the subject, too: "All health and success does me good, however far off and withdrawn it may appear."

In medieval lore there was a belief that the life of a saint redeemed his entire village, opening heaven's gates for its inhabitants. This belief is at the root of the practice of collecting relics in village churches. It is akin to the cabalistic belief in the presence of "twelve righteous men" whose piety redeems the world. No one knows who the men might be, not even the men themselves.

This may be the best argument, apart from the charitable works it might do, for aligning with a religious group—although it can be detrimental if we quit thinking.

January 11: * We still have a war of ideas between Hellenism, represented by Pan (instincts), and Hebrewism, represented by Christ. One is natural; one is ideal. Matthew Arnold, in his essay, "Hebrewism and Hellenism," wrote, "The governing idea of Hebrewism is strictness of conscience. That of Hellenism is spontaneity of consciousness." One lives in "caves obscure," the other has the Mount. One has music, the other has the Word. Pan's legs are crooked, hairy and his feet are cloven-hoofed. Jesus' legs are broken and his feet are crossed and nailed. Pan is the unruly goat, while Jesus is the Good Shepherd. Pan is naked and phallic while Jesus is circumcised, covered and asexual.

Early Christianity, borrowing from Judaism, brought the suppression of natural urges, represented by Pan, who soon became the goat-footed Devil. His habitat was always dells, grottos, woods and wilds—never villages or cities. He was a shepherd's god (also a metaphor used by Jesus). In one account Pan was fathered by Aether, the invisible substance that is *everywhere*. In Homer's *Hymn to Pan*, he was abandoned at birth by his wood-nymph mother. His father, Hermes, wrapped him in a hare's pelt and took him to Olympus where he was accepted by all *(pan)* the gods, particularly Dionysos (Dionysus), the god of revelry.

The hare was particularly sacred to Aphrodite, Eros, the Bacchic world, and the moon, so Pan was "wrapped" in those associations. Then Hermes (the messenger) gave him qualities that made his actions promptings from nature. In other words, he was a chthonic spirit; his actions were connections that *meant* something.

But we no longer heed nature. With Pan dead, so was his alter-ego, Echo (reflection), and we could no longer capture consciousness through reflecting within our instincts. When Pan is dead, then nature can be controlled by the will, modeled in the image of Prometheus or Hercules, creating from it and polluting it without conscious.

The problem is that the "spirit of Pan" is very much alive.In nightmares repressed nature returns. What we have disowned as unworthy reappears as shadow figures in our dreams. When ego sleeps, instinctual levels of fear, aggression, hunger or sexuality produce images that take on lives of their own. The imaginal world is alive with animism. The world is imaged by different "gods" with attributes and characteristics, which is polytheistic *pan*theism. *In sleep one understands that fear, dread, horror are natural,*no matter how much we deny them. This is deep, instinctual wisdom.

January 12: * The earliest known alphabetic writing has been discovered by John C. Darnell, a Yale Egyptologist, along an ancient desert road in Egypt. Carved inscriptions place the invention of the alphabet at around 2000 B.C., about three centuries earlier, and in a different country, than had been previously thought. Semitic-speaking people working in Egypt had simplified about 27 hieroglyphs and assigned them tiny sounds of speech. Around 1000 B.C. this evolved into the Phoenician alphabet.

And how about this? The letters J and V were accepted as full-fledged letters just 200 years ago! Julius Caesar was really Iulius.

January 13: * Now I understand better about Catholic icons. Unless an incident is made concrete, it does not happen in the psyche, because the unconscious doesn't understand abstracts. It has to be thought about, then written about, painted, danced, sung, or played as music to register in the unconscious. It must move from literal to metaphoric if it is to be assimilated. This part of ourself cannot read; it isn't abstract. It lives on concreteness, on symbol, on metaphor, on image. My teacher in symbols class, Veniece Standley, said often: "You have to put it into matter before the unconscious understands it."

Western philosophical tradition from its beginnings in the Pre-Socratics and the Old Testament, has been prejudiced against images *(phantasia),* favoring instead thought-abstractions. The psyche's tendency to personify has been put down as anthropomorphism. It isn't so much that we personify, but that the epiphanies come in our dreams, not as rational thoughts, but as persons or animals.

For millennia, divine and daimonic figures appeared as persons. Herodotus recounts how Pan burst in on Pheidippides to give him a crucial message that saved Athens and thus the origin of democracy. The Athenians believed Pheidippides' message, won the battle, and set up the Cult of Pan in Athens. Charles Boer writes, "This was one of the greatest moments in the history of Western civilization, this apparition of a goat-footed God on the eve of a world-transforming battle, his message of help actually making a momentous difference in events that led to saving democracy itself."

Jung, understanding how the psyche works, went against the current of the times by identifying *images* as the primary data of the psyche. Then he took those images at their sensual, emotional level. His movement away from abstract concept toward feelings corresponds with the movement from intellect to imagination.

January 14: * Creativity is play. When we are so closely related to the imagination, we're constantly creating. But there's no creativity without being able to surrender. There is a fine line between surrender of the will and total surrender of the ego. In *The Prelude,* Wordsworth writes: "Imagination.../ Is but another name for absolute power...." If this absolute power of the imagination overwhelms our reason, we are left a lunatic.

* When I was a kid, the Pledge of Allegiance was: "I pledge allegiance to the flag and to the republic for which it stands: one nation, indivisible, with liberty and justice for all." This was adopted on October 13, 1892, and that's the way it stayed until 1942, when it was amended to include "of the United States." It wasn't until 1954 that "under God" was added.

January 15: * Our parents set standards and we tried to live up to their expectations. We learn to perform rather than to be ourselves, so our soul goes into hiding. As adults, we wonder, "Whom should I please so as to make the best performance?" After trying to please everyone, we begin to ask, "Wait a minute. Who am I? What about *my* needs?" Sometimes point people find themselves on a suicidal journey. Their perfectionist ideals have lured them from their own life. Having lost the sheer joy of being alive, they live by will power.

One man spent hours in front of the mirror, trimming every little hair, examining every detail of his appearance, checking the impeccable shine of his shoes, because "A good appearance is a silent recommendation." (A paraphrase of Pubilius Syrus: "A fair exterior is a silent recommendation.") But if we become so obsessed with outward appearance that we lose our core, we are no longer able to express anything but what we think people want to hear.

January 16: * Here's knowledge I wonder how I have lived so long without: In Scotland, gamekeepers get to keep the stags' pizzles. (Figure it out.) Each complete set weighs up to 2.2 pounds and after they have been ground together, they are much prized in the Far East for their libido-improving properties. The stalkers, gamekeepers and ghillies swap pizzle stories in the bothies over a peaty fire while they enjoy a dram. (A wee dram, spot or tot is 25 ml. In America, if you order a blet, blast, shot, slug or snort, you get at least 50 ml.)

January 17: * The word "pagan" comes from the Latin *paganus*, meaning "civilian," as opposed to *miles*, meaning "soldier." Later it came to mean "heathen," that is, not Christian. So now "pagan practices" are considered terrible, which is peculiar, given the survival of so many of them—including many, many Christmas traditions—from prehistoric times into our own. In 601 a pragmatic Pope Gregory I, who was dispatching Abbot Mellitus to Britain, sent along a letter for Bishop Augustine that said, in part, "I have come to the conclusion that the temples of the idols in England should not on any account be destroyed. Augustine must smash the idols, but the temples themselves should be sprinkled with holy water and altars set up in them....For we ought to take advantage of well-built temples by purifying them from devil-worship...."

* Pawnee Chief Letakots said this in 1904 (recorded by Natalie Curtis): "In the beginning of all things, wisdom and knowledge were with the animals; for Tirawa, the One Above, did not speak directly to man. He sent certain animals to tell men that he showed himself through the beasts, and from them, and the stars and the sun and the moon, man should learn. Tirawa spoke to man through his works."

January 18: * Sometimes I delude myself that the past is gone, but it just isn't so. The crossroads in Europe still have little cairns where people drop their stones in honor of the goddess, the oldest earth mother, in Greek myth, named Hecate. A crossroads represents a place where consciousness is crossed by unconsciousness, where the eternal crosses the transitory. Places and times, in other words, when we must surrender our egos to something higher.

By this time, old earth mother has been down every road. She's seen it all, been buffeted by every wind. She's got nothing to lose. She can be exactly who she is, and who she is can't be taken from her. She has no investment in ego, so there's no hidden agenda operating. She can afford to be honest because there's no one to impress. She's not playing games anymore. People trust her and are brought into harmony with her. It's refreshing not to play games.

January 19: * Many of our earliest links with our forebears have been paved over. But in Scotland's Orkney Islands, it's believed that the oldest extant houses, possibly in northwestern Europe, are the two at Knap of Howar on Papa Westray. They are interconnected long houses dating between 3600 and 3100 B.C. There is a kitchen with a central hearth and a living room, separated by walls of thin stone slabs. There is an entrance space that once had a wooden doorway, leading from a farm workshop with storage cupboards and shelves. Very little except thousands of years, separates us.

* The Thirteen Colonies were not religiously tolerant. Massachusetts, a Puritan theocracy in 1660, hanged many Quakers. Maryland had a major problem with Puritans. Another would not allow Baptists to marry. Roger Williams, founder of Rhode Island, was the father of complete separation of church and state, because any religion with government support has an advantage over other religions and at times becomes deadly to members of other religions.

January 20: * Why haven't we snapped to this before? We're so convinced our belief is the right one and there can be only *one* right one, we will go to war to *force* someone else to believe as we do. It never works by force. Nobody can step into our circle and try to change our beliefs, any more than we can violate someone else's circle. We're not in charge.

Here's an example: Before there was a Scotland, there were four kingdoms there. One was Daldriada. One was Pictavia, whose capital was Old Scone. The present Scone Palace, seat of the Earls of Mansfield, is located on the site of the eighth century capital and is a few miles northeast of Perth. A high place nearby, called Mote or Moot Hill, was a meeting place and was originally called *Tom-a-mhoid*, meaning "the hill where justice is administered." In 710 Pict King Naitan renamed it "Castle of Belief" and announced that Easter and the resurrection would henceforth be observed in Pictavia. This pronouncement led to a quarrel with the Dalriadics, who believed nothing of the kind, a quarrel which lasted for many years.

Throughout history, wars have been fought because one group attempted to force their religious beliefs upon another people. Change in belief *does* happen, but never with that current generation or the subsequent one. New generations far removed will see things differently. In the case of the Picts and Daldriads, the wars lasted well over a century—133 years. By modern standards, that's more than six generations; at that time it was at least seven! Finally, in *c.*843-844, under Daldriadic King Kenneth mac Alpin, the two kingdoms made a pact and Alba (later Scotland) was born.

January 21: * A sign of middle age: when we no longer measure our lives in years since our birth but now estimate the unknowable number of years left before death. The attainment of a new stage of life demands that initiation symbols appropriate to that stage must be experienced. The symbol for this step might be the minus sign. ("Life consists of subtractions, things we have to give up," Lucie Delarue Mardus said.) No matter how we try to avoid it, each hour nibbles at our solidity, and we grudgingly relinquish something in every little humiliation. An early Jungian, Florida Scott-Maxwell, said of this level, "Though we are aching, inadequate wrecks, there are times when, in our hearts, we are incurably, deliciously young." During this transitional period, the words from *Tao Te Ching* are apt: "Give up your knowledge, then you shall be free from care!"

In the Gnostic creation myth, *Nous* is a spark of the Divine that breaks free from the Upper Regions and, looking down from Heaven, he sees his own reflection mirrored back from far below in the dark chaos of *Physis*, the essence of matter. *Physis,* out of her own longing, opens herself and welcomes this spark into her depths. Joining, they bring about the first Creation. A spark of something numinous impregnates the vast unformed darkness of the unconscious, gestating new understanding. During a time of liminality and confusion, we await this birth with joy but also with dread of the unknown.

Every pregnant woman knows this feeling. Every stage of life is a new creation.

January 22: * The clash between Middle East and West is like old war-loving gods riding to battle in the skies. Sometimes we believe we can see a situation more clearly than someone else, and we're tempted to play god and exert our will over him/her. I'm reminded of the ambitious Icarus, who fashioned wings of wax so that he could see the divine sun, but he flew too close, the heat melted the wax on his wings, and he fell to earth. Myths tell us that those who experience the radiance of the gods are often burned to cinders by the encounter. Just to be our human selves is excitement enough.

January 23: * For the first time since the Ice Age, the Polar Ice Cap in Siberia has melted, uncovering 11,000-year-old peat bogs. These are emitting tons of methane gas into the atmosphere, further accelerating global warming, nobody knows how fast. This may not be the earth's worst warming period, but it could be.

The warm Atlantic waters in 2005 produced more tropical storms than any other year on record. When Katrina devastated the Gulf Coast, many countries, even those which opposed Bush's preemptory war on Iraq, offered aid to the U.S., but Germany's environment minister, Jürgen Trittin, commented, in effect, "You asked for it." Writing in the *Frankfurter Rundschau* newspaper, he said George W. Bush (who had refused to join the rest of the industrialized nations to sign the Kyoto Protocol to lower atmospheric gasses that limit production of climate-warming greenhouse gasses) and his corporate cronies had brought this on themselves. He suggested the hurricane's severity was at least partly a result of current global warming: "[T]he American president is closing his eyes to the economic and human costs" of shunning the Kyoto Protocol. The problem is that natural disasters rarely touch corporate big dogs.

January 24: * A recurring theme in fairy tale and legend is that the hero flees when asked to kiss the loathsome maiden or the serpent queen. Each night she pleads for his embrace. Each time he refuses, her form becomes more terrifying; she grows more heads, more scales, more girth. Finally the hero's youngest brother is courageous enough to kiss her or make love to her, whereupon she is transformed into a beautiful woman who then bestows upon him dominion over a vast kingdom. This tale is told throughout the world. Only the one willing to embrace what is dark, archaic and terrifying can become a wise ruler, servant to the Queen (of Nature).

The tale also has a flip version, in which it is the princess who must kiss the frog or something even more disgusting.

(Who said, "A man must swallow a toad each morning to be certain of not encountering something more loathsome before the day is over."? Sounds like an Englishman. Michael Moncurs' *Cynical Quotations* puts it this way: "Eat a live toad the first thing in the morning and nothing worse will happen to you the rest of the day." —but lists the author as unknown.)

A major task of coming to old age is to acknowledge and embrace our embodiment, our primitive saurian (lizard-like) being.

But we also have a spiritual nature that can emanate unconditional love. We have divine qualities: love, wisdom, strength, compassion, patience, and faith to overcome any challenge. These qualities *must* be divine, for they are not like us otherwise.

January 25: * Seven U.S. presidents had connections to the same man: John Bowne, who settled in New York in the 1600s. They are: John Adams, John Quincy Adams, Abraham Lincoln, Richard M. Nixon, Gerald Ford, George H. W. Bush, and George W. Bush. Four mayors of New York City were also connected to Bowne: John Lawrence, Maarinus Willett, Walter Bowne, and Cornelius Lawrence.

* Dubai, that most modern of cities, has adapted some of our TV programs, one being "The Apprentice." But Arabic is fond of formal indirectness, so the producers replaced Trumps blunt, humiliating "You're fired!" with a line that translates, "May God be kind to you."

January 26: * When I was around nine, sitting on a horse at my neighbor's house, I had an epiphany: I realized how lucky I was to have been born, first, white—because the black people in my town had a very hard time—and second, a girl, because girls didn't have to go to work but could stay home and do any number of things that were more fun than sitting at a desk. They could garden or sew or grocery shop or wah and iron or play with babies or cook. They could play the piano and sing and dance any time they wanted to, all of which my daddy loved to do, but he had to go to work.

But my attitudes about "women's work" gradually changed when I realized how little it was respected. The dominance of masculine values through so many centuries has had a dangerous effect on the psyche of both genders. Even the so-called "women's movement" was antagonistic, confrontational, and divisive: characteristics of masculine ways of operating.

Psychologist say that man fears, thus despises, his own inferior feminine side, so woman has learned to despise her dominant value, her femininity. This attitude persists in the unconscious long after it has changed consciously. Many women project the feminine values onto trivial vanities or onto what they call "domestic drudgery," the very things I thought looked like so much fun. Because traditional feminine duties have been devalued, we as a society have lost our soul. There's no one to tend the sacred hearth with its spark of the divine or to bring to humanity its understanding of its divinity. Thus we women identify womanhood with a despised aspect of the *anima* and fail to recognize our true identity as carriers of relatedness, feeling values, the quiet nourishing qualities of the earth.

Incidentally, back on that day when I was sitting on the horse, I also thought I was so lucky to live in the best town in the best state in the best country on earth. I was grown before I realized that my "best town" was in the heart of the Dust Bowl, and that according to history books, I was supposed to have been miserable.

January 27: * On intellectualism, the explanation to *I Ching* hexagram 30 says in part: "Clarity of mind has the same relation to life as fire has to wood. Fire clings to wood but also consumes it. Clarity of mind is rooted in life but can also consume it." The course of my life depends on the nature of the fuel I feed my being. When the fuel is provided by an ego dominated by desire, particularly unconscious desire, the fire will be a straw fire, flaring up quickly in emotional reactions, power drives, or intellectual ambitions, transforming nothing. Line 3 of the hexagram says, "In the light of the setting sun men either beat the pot and sing or loudly bewail the approach of old age."

January 28: * Italian analyst Aldo Carotenuto says myth is a way of responding to the apparent absurdity of existence. It brings order to chaos and forms the first nucleus of what will later be the *meaning* of life. (Psychologist Jean Houston said, "A myth is something that never happened that is always happening.") Myths naturally evolved during the course of history. At least a portion of myth is the unconscious self-representation of the development of consciousness.

* Steven Leacock: "Fair weather is God's gift to the plain people who feel that they have to be eating dill pickle on the highway. But rainy weather was made for the philosophers."

January 29: * In fairy tales the good fairy or helpful animal turns up when the hero performs an act of courage. It is an illusion to think that help is necessary *before* we can make a move. Generally the opposite is true. The assistance comes at the moment we face up to the danger or the challenge alone.

* Yvonne Nelson Perry: "A family is a long chain of people. Someone holds onto you, you hold onto someone, and that person holds onto someone else. If everyone holds tight, you always know who you are."

January 30: * Jung defines synchronicity as "a meaningful coincidence of two or more events, where something other than the probability of chance in involved." Arthur Koestler traces the idea of synchronicity back to the Pythagorean harmony of the spheres and the Hippocratics' "sympathy of all things." Koestler says, "There is one common flow, one common breathing, all things are in sympathy....telepathy, clairvoyance, precognition...and synchronicity are merely different manifestations under different conditions of the same universal principle—i.e., the integrative tendency operating through both causal and acausal agencies."

* Attention poets: The Greek poet Horace said, "No verse can give pleasure for long, nor last, that is written by water-drinkers."

January 31: * I'm thinking about a Chilean woman who said, in a book I compiled called *Letters from Women Around the World*: "I was beginning to think I would live my whole life through, and nobody would ever hear the sound of my voice."

A similar feeling must be behind the reaction to a new national project called StoryCorps which encourages people to record interviews with their parents for the Library of Congress' American Folklife Center. The idea to record the oral histories of everyday Americans was the brainchild of radio documentarian Dave Isay, who says that often when the mike is turned on, people start to cry. "They feel so honored people actually want to listen."

This sympathy for those who, like the Chilean woman, are afraid to die without ever being heard, has been the motivation for much of what I have done since compiling that book.

February

February 1: * The tradition of Spring Cleaning has its roots in ancient Rome, where the New Year began in March. Prior to its arrival, a general cleansing took place, and the entire last month of the old year was named for the utensils used for cleaning: the *februa*. It is not unlike the cardinal building its nest. I well remember, prior to the birth of my first child, I waxed the floors to our small apartment nine times in one week! That was spring cleaning gone berserk. Floors, in Jungian symbols, might connote one's standpoint. If so, I was about to change mine in a grand way, and I was preparing my ground of being.

* The Celtic holiday Imbolc was the first day of February. It celebrated calving, lambing, and the start of sowing. Cocks were sacrificed where three streams met, using only white birds. It was once also called the Feast of Brigantia, who was the Celtic goddess of fertility.

February 2: * To coincide with the Celtic holiday Imbolc, the Christians introduced a service of consecration for all candles to be used throughout the year, in memory of the purification of the Virgin Mary. Thus arose the name Candlemas Day, which is still printed in our journals on February 2. An old Scottish proverb says:

If Candlemas Day be dry and fair,
The half o' winter's to come and mair;
If Candlemas Day be wet and foul,
The half o' winter has gone at Youl.

February 3: * I once heard Adela Rogers St. John say that in ancient times, marble columns and pottery items were inspected for flaws, which were filled in with wax before being glazed. Those that were flawless, therefore were "sine cera" or without wax, which some philogists suggest has become, in English, "sincere." Now I learn to my disappointment that the word "sincere" actually derives from the Latin "sincerus," meaning "sound" or "uncorrupt."

* Psyche: the presence of the observer in the things observed, a presence that changes what is observed. When we see something

"out there" we see an image. The consciousness of the image as an image is what is meant by soul. Soul is not bound to the external thing. Soul is the world of metaphor. Artists know it, and when they lose the metaphor-making power, they know it in the most intimate, immediate and painful sense. William Blake called the body "that portion of Soul discerned by the five senses."

February 4: * Michaelangelo's first important work was the Pietà, the only work he ever signed. I always thought he painted the fresco on the ceiling of the Sistine Chapel while lying on his back, but I read that he stood on scaffolding and painted over his head.

Before we moved to Montgomery County we were warned that its population had the average I.Q. of a radish. This turned out to be false, with the exception of at least one woman who raised a stink because a replica of Michaelangelo's David was erected in a shopping center. Her protests probably led the poor radish to take offense at the comparison. One hopes she never goes to Italy or even to Houston's Museum of Fine Art, where she would find plenty of nudes to offend her. Robert Pinsky, poet laureate (1997-2000), writes eloquently about the two-fold nature of the provincial town: the aridity, the constricting yet enabling life, the supportive human scale of a small community and its stifling mores and isolation from history.

February 5: * The dead of winter is an ideal time for introspection. If we live day by day, in touch with the world around us, even one minute a day, as Blake says, that's the moment in each day Satan cannot find us. It's what we need to keep the soul alive. During the rest of the year, we keep very busy to avoid hearing the messages that body and soul are trying to send us. When the body sends distress signals, we prefer to pretend nothing is happening, or that there will be a new drug or technological advance to take care of the problem at the last minute—as if the body were somehow separate from who we are. We go to great lengths to keep from listening to our inner voices. We're afraid of silence because in silence we experience nothingness. The imagination is dormant. We keep the radio or telly going like wallpaper for the rest of our lives to cover the emptiness. Even when we're jogging, we've got music in our ears.

We live for the most part in a state of denial, running from ourselves for fear we might discover that deep down, there's nobody home. So the dark of winter is a gift that allows us a moment to stop and find ourselves.

February 6: * A recent study says class is a potent force in health and longevity in the U.S. The more education and income people have, the less likely they are to have and die of heart disease, strokes, diabetes and many types of cancer. Upper-middle-class Americans live longer and in better health than middle-class Americans, who live longer and better than those at the bottom. And the gaps are widening, say people who have researched social factors in health.

As advances in medicine and disease prevention have increased life expectancy in the United States, the benefits have disproportionately gone to people with education, money, good jobs and connections. They are almost invariably in the best position to learn new information early, modify their behavior, take advantage of the latest treatments and have the cost covered by insurance.

** We are the only industrialized nation on the planet that doesn't guarantee access to medical care for every man, woman, and child.*

February 7: * In sacred ritual, since ancient times, the ego crosses into sacred space and surrenders to the divine. When the god enters, the ego opens and expands; it has touched the timeless world that gives meaning to this one. The mystery, the magic of the experience stays with the ego, enriching it, giving new perspective to the everyday world. But for most people today, science has tainted their belief in mystery. Their current religious tradition no longer holds the numinosity, the light, the consciousness that enriches the soul.

February 8: * Interesting word derivation: The distilled brew *uisge-breatha* or *usquebaugh* ("water of life") eventually became known by the word "whisky."

Until the arrival of the hydrometer in 1740, the way to test "proof" of whisky was with gunpowder, which was mixed with the whisky. If the gunpowder flashed, that meant there was sufficient whisky to allow ignition, and thus it was "proved."

February 9: * We grew up with the idea that it's the white hats against the black ones, as if there were two camps of people in the world. Gradually, the black hats seemed to grow in number until finally we come to the point where we're the only white hat standing. We come to be quite sure the black hats are somehow sub-human. We believe that because we can't see their souls, they don't have them. It's a tricky thing to see the soul of another person. It's an impossibility without love. The soul learned long ago that if it shows itself, it will get knocked down. That begins in childhood, when the child's soul tries to express itself and the parent says, "You shouldn't think that. That's not how you feel."

Our culture is terrified of passion because at the core, people have been treated with power. When the parent says, "What are you thinking about?" the child quickly learns to say, "Nothing." To do otherwise would be a leap into darkness, to say in effect, "I trust you to let me live." When the parent says, "Where are you going?" the teenager says, "Out." The child is saying, "I don't trust you anymore." At the root of the fear of passion is fear of our inner rage against those who ignored our boundaries and made us do what they wanted us to do, made us think what they believed we should think. This rage is a forbidden, terrifying thing that is not to be tolerated or recognized, lest it possess us completely. It may not be confined to rage against parental authority; it may travel with us through life, so that at a subliminal level, we carry rage against our spouse or our boss, our political leaders.

February 10: * D. H. Lawrence asked, "Are you willing to be sponged out, erased, canceled, made nothing…dipped in oblivion? If not, you will never really change." But who is to say that someone must change? Change into what? Someone else's estimation of what one must be? Well, time says that we *must* change. When we notice that it has crept up on us unawares, we seek to turn life around, to redeem all our failures before we get too old. But we must sacrifice even that desire. Only if we can give up our brightest hopes is *metanoia* possible.

February 11: * Marion Woodman describes a time when she was very ill and had decided that life wasn't worth living. Finally she perceived her body as if it were a loyal dog lying on the ground. She thought, "He's waiting for me to come back, just like my own little dog would wait." She wouldn't betray her own dog, but she was betraying her own body. She had been given a life and had had almost betrayed it. She was overcome by the sweetness of this patient thing, her body, trusting that she would come back. She decided to take responsibility for her life because it wasn't hers to throw away.

February 12: * Another kind of grace: Modern chaos theory, specifically, the second law of thermodynamics, holds that all energy structures eventually run down. But British physicist Ian Prigogine found a contrary situation in nature where chaos induces, instead of collapse and complete breakdown, a jump to a higher level of complexity: a surprising capacity for self-organization in certain "dissipative structures." If the tension of a system in distress is held until a certain critical mass is achieved, rather than breaking down, the system evolves to a higher level! A new pattern is created.

Hegel thought that thesis and antithesis wrestle in unending conflict until a third thing, a synthesis, emerges, seemingly of its own accord. In other words, if the tension of opposites is held long enough, a third thing emerges: a transcendent function, according to Carl Jung: a *tertium non datur*, meaning the third not known. The conflict of opposites giving rise to a third thing can be felt as grace in action. Out of the ashes, the phoenix rises.

February 13: * On this date in 1692, the Massacre of Glencoe (Scotland) occurred, all because the chief of the MacIan MacDonalds clan was too late in swearing an oath of loyalty to William of Orange. A party led by Robert Campbell of Glen Lyon killed 38 people, including MacIan and his wife. The nine of diamonds in a pack of playing cards is often known as "The curse of Scotland." The person who initiated the attack at Glencoe was John Dalrymple, Secretary of State for Scotland at the time, and Master of Stair. Dalrymple's coat of arms boasts nine lozenges. (Could he be a distant relation of Terry Dalrymple, who teaches English at Angelo State U. and wrote a collection of fiction called *Salvation and Other Stories*?)

* There is another version of the story as to why the nine of diamonds is called "the curse of Scotland": After the Battle of Culloden, the Duke of Cumberland wrote down on a playing card,

which happened to be the nine of diamonds, his orders for the slaughter of all Jacobites, wherever they were found.

February 14: * The root of the word "free" is "pri," meaning "love." "Pri" is also the origin of "friend," and of the name of the Nordic goddess of love, "Frigg," (also Frigga) and of her day, Friday.

* Here we are at St. Valentine's Day, the holiday that all husbands wish had never been invented.

February 15: * In the wisdom of ancient China and Japan, the serpent/dragon was considered a symbol of creativity. Those who were visited by one in their dreams were considered blessed, and much was expected of them in return.

* The leaves of the aspen and the cottonwood, I learned in a poem by Robert Haas, flutter and turn because in the heat of summer, that motion protects its cells from drying out.

February 16: * T. S. Eliot details three gifts reserved for age. First are the changes taking place in the body. The losses we incur may deprive us of much of the "enchantment" we have taken for granted as a channel of meaning.

The second is "helpless rage at the terrifying folly of men" and of their laughter at things which are not even faintly amusing, but tragically serious. Only creative imagination finds the place beyond rage, which is compassion and joy.

The third is memories, that grow stronger and more vivid with age. Eliot says painful memories are gifts which bring us the crown of life. The loss of energy and enchantment, the rage of projection of our hidden faults onto others, or onto circumstances, the suffering hidden in our memories, become the essentials of liberation. Love is born that frees us from both past and future. Eliot's image of that freedom is the dance. Shakespeare's word for this dance is "mercy."

Through memories re-experienced as story, our life begins to move in a circle around the still point of the Center. It is a small pattern, unique and constant, in the dance of creation.

Now comes the faint dawning of the awareness of the unity of all things, harmonizing with the great "unstruck sound." It sounds though the entire universe.

"Enchantment" means "filled with chant," or song, so when we come to be aware of the unstruck sound, there will indeed be true enchantment.

February 17: * *Uroboros* is a Greek word that refers to the Egyptian alchemical figure of the serpent biting its own tail. It is a perfect circle, enclosed in itself and self-sufficient. Its circular movement is paradoxically the expression of immobility and passivity, but at the same time the portent of an imminent creation.

* Sheila D. Collins: "Racism, sexism, class exploitation and ecological destruction are four interlocking pillars upon which the structure of the patriarchy rests."

February 18: * Aldo Cartenuto contends that "men are for the most part extremely superficial in their feelings" because from childhood, the male child already feels his own diversity from the mother. He is thus in a greater hurry to emerge from the maternal world and to distance himself from it, even violently if necessary, to make his way to the patriarchal world. The time he spends within a fundamental relationship such as with his mother is much shorter, and this imprinting, for all its necessity, helps to make the adult male virtually incapable for forming true relationships. Like Odysseus, he never commits himself, and he must always move on because he cannot dwell in any situation.

In that older paradigm, the man was set apart from the rest of the family and showed his manliness by being tough-minded and tough-willed, never admitting he didn't know or could be mistaken. Expressing emotion was not part of that paradigm. He had to be the authority on everything. It must have been secretly stressful for that man, who had to keep up a show of strength that he didn't always feel. It would've been a great relief to admit a weakness.

February 19: * In the course of growing older, we pass from a situation of complete adherence to our parents to gradually taking a stand against them—at least temporarily. The truth is, we are much more conditioned by our early environment than we generally care to admit. We always carry within us our basic condition.

Social deliverance generally occurs through study. Those who come from a deprived childhood must make an enormous effort to bridge the gap and actually travel much farther than those who were closer to the goal at birth. Those who are born where no paths have been laid out go to immense difficulties to find their own.

The myth of the hero is always present, with its three fundamental points: the hero (the evolving ego), the dragon (what stands in the way of our growth), and the treasure (goal that is difficult to reach, always related to the birth of a new stage in our growth.) Every time life imposes a change, we face a "dragon" that guards our treasure and must be fought. In Jungian terms, the fight with the dragon, to "kill the mother" and "kill the father" represents our struggle to grow up, form our own opinions, make our own decisions. It is much easier to turn around than to face the dragon.

February 20: * If we lived in Roman times, we would be celebrating Parentalia now. Ancient Romans prefaced the beginning of the New Year (March 1) by a prolonged adoration of the dead, culminating in the nine-day festival of Parentalia, or Departed Ancestors. Purple flowers were strewn on their graves, and offerings to them were placed under the thresholds, to welcome them when they re-entered their former homes on March 1.

February 21: * The compulsive part of ourselves is an evil energy that wants to rob us of our life. The compulsively neat person neglects his relationships while attempting to bring perfect order into his world, to *control* his surroundings. When we face this compulsion directly, its negative power constellates against us, trying to dissuade us from doing anything about it.

There's a difference between being compulsively neat and simply keeping our lives orderly. We maintain order in our everyday lives when we complete simple tasks such as organizing a drawer, cleaning a closet, or putting things in their places. This is a reflection of a greater, divine order that we tap into when we clear the clutter of negativity from our minds and make room for divine ideas to enter.

February 22: * The root of the word "mercy" is probably the Etruscan *merc*, from which both "commerce" and "merchant" are derived. It's therefore connected with basic images of exchange.

Mercy is compassion, suffering *with* all creation. It takes us beyond the need for specific pardon. When the greatest wrongs we have suffered, even our own worst faults, are known at last as indeed the saving grace (the refining fire of which Eliot writes in "Little Gidding,"), then pardon or being forgiven has no more relevance.

February 23: * *Metanoia* comes from a Greek word meaning "a fundamental shift of mind." There is extraordinary power in a group committed to a common vision. If we could learn to dialogue with each other at a deep level, we would find ways to relate to one another that would dissolve the perception of separateness. Relatively few people working together in this way could have a profound effect on society because, according to physicist David Bohm, their consciousness is woven into all consciousness.

All matter, like the entire universe, is continually in motion. At a level we cannot see, there is an unbroken wholeness, an "implicate order," out of which seemingly discrete events arise. As part of the universe, human beings are part of that unbroken whole with is continually unfolding. When you meet someone who insists on the status quo, run away as fast as you can.

The universe is linked by a fabric of invisible connections. Small changes at the right place can have a systemwide impact, because these changes share the unbroken wholeness that unites the entire system. A seemingly insignificant act in one part of the whole creates nonlocal results that may emerge far away. Unseen connections create effects at a distance (quantum leaps).

When I have an "original idea," like picnicking in a remote spot, soon I learn half the population thought of it, too, and the spot isn't remote anymore.

Scientists have begun to speak in terms of "fields" to explain connections they observe. David Bohm speaks of the "general fielding" for all mankind: "We are all connected and operate within living fields of thought and perception."

Rupert Sheldrake, a British biologist working on field theory, has defined fields as nonmaterial regions of influence: invisible forces that structure space or behavior. There are fundamental quantum matter fields recognized by physicists–electron fields, neutron fields, etc. They are invisible, intangible, inaudible, tasteless, odorless, and yet in quantum theory, they are the substance of the universe. Fields are states of space, but space is full of energy and invisible structures that interconnect.

So the immeasurable "things" are actually what is most real. We live in a relational, participative universe. What is unfolding in the world is unique. This is an "open" moment in history. In the rich countries, the paradox of prosperity and deteriorating public services, congestion, dirtier cities, rising crime, pollution cause a basic rethinking of the growth paradigm. Quality of life becomes a primary issue, and growth for its own sake is not necessarily desirable.

But small discontinuities can suddenly transform the whole system significantly. We have enormous opportunities to create something new. By working together, thinking together, building shared mental models, we can contribute to the healthy, peaceful environment we want to see unfolding.

February 24: * The wise among the ancients of every civilization have been aware of the dangers of civilizing oneself through the willful repression of the old, animal self. It is dangerous to ignore the existence of the irrational. We have many versions of what happens to those who cross Dionysus, who deny the lasciviousness, barbarism, sadism, darkness at the root of their own souls.

Our modern-day version of radical conservative religionists in more than one society, obsessed with piety, repression of sexual urges, duty, loyalty and sacrifice, yet willing to commit the most heinous, savage crimes and visit utter destruction upon their fellow humans in the name of bringing "morality" to the world, are at some level not only frightened of evil but also terribly attracted to it.

The more cultivated a person is, the more he needs some channel through which to vent the primitive impulses he's worked so hard to subdue. Otherwise, those powerful old forces will mass and strengthen until they are violent enough to break free, more violent for the delay, often strong enough to sweep away the will entirely.

(The caged animal is the most dangerous.)

February 25: * It has been observed that the oddest tongues, the strangest mythologies, the oldest cities, the most barbarous religions, come from landscapes of broken, wild terrain. In myth, Pan and

Zeus were both born in the mountains.

In these oldest of places, we can see that hierarchies were a method of group survival. This must have grown out of the hive concept, where drones and workers happily accept their place in society because to do otherwise would be to jeopardize the queen, which would in turn mean the death of the hive.

In Plato's *Republic*, justice in a society is when each level of hierarchy works within its place and is content with it. The rub has come with the hubristic notion in modern society that the lower levels of the hierarchy are somehow dispensable, somehow less important. (Take women's lib, for instance, which for a while downplayed the importance of the stay-at-home mom.) Many great civilizations have buried themselves by succumbing to this notion.

February 26: * There are certain ideas common to a people which become inexpressible in another tongue. Hence, the borrowing from other languages to express these concepts. Look at fire: An *Incendium* is different from the *feu* with which the Frenchman lights his cigarette, and both are not the same as the stark, inhuman *pur* of the ancient Greeks, that bright and terrible clarity that roared from the towers of Ilion or leaped and screamed on that desolate, windy beach, from the funeral pyre of Patroklos.

February 27: * King Alfred the Great (849-c. 900) had the 450 B.C. laws of Celtic king Dunwal Molmutius (son of Cloton, Duke of Cornwall—Shakespeare called Molmutius the first king of Britain) translated from the Celtic so that he could incorporate them into his Anglo-Saxon Code. Molmutius had in turn, according to Strabo, based his laws on the code of the druid Brutus (C. 1100 B.C.) The following extracts show the enduring legacy of the ancient druids a thousand years before the time of Christ on our lives today, and lead us to question: *who is/was the more civilized:*

~ There are three tests of civil liberty: equality of rights, equality of taxation, and freedom to come and go.

~ There are three causes which ruin a state: inordinate privileges, corruption of justice, and national apathy.

~ There are three things which cannot be considered solid longer than their foundations are solid: peace, property, and law.

~ There are three things free to all Britons: the forest, the unworked mine, and the right of hunting wild creatures.

~ There are three things that require the unanimous vote of the nation to effect: deposition of the sovereign, introduction of novelties in religion, and suspension of the law.

~ There are three civil birthrights to every Briton: the right to go wherever he pleases, the right, wherever he is, to protection from his land and sovereign, and the right of equal privileges and equal restrictions.

~ There are three property birthrights of every Briton: five (British) acres of land for a home, the right of armoral bearings, and the right of suffrage in the enacting of laws—the male at twenty-one, the female on her marriage. *(I find this particularly interesting, since as late as January 12, 1915, the U.S. House of Representatives rejected a proposal to give women the right to vote.)*

~ There are three guarantees of society: security for life and limb, security for the property, and security of the rights of nature.

~ There are three things which every Briton may legally be compelled to attend: the worship of God, military service, and the courts at law.

~ There are three things free to every man, Briton or foreigner: water from spring, river or well, fire from a decayed tree, and a block of stone not in use.

~ There are three orders who are exempt from bearing arms: the bard, the judge, and the graduate in law or religion.

~ Three persons who have a right to public maintenance: the old, the babe, and the foreigner who cannot speak the British tongue.

February 28: * The so-called "classless society" that our forefathers envisioned has morphed into many strata, to our everlasting disgrace. Even some of the signers of the Declaration of Independence were slave holders. Our models for a democratic society, reaching back into Greek times, leave out the fact that the Greeks had slaves, and democracy was only for the land owners—men only, to boot. We borrowed our legal ideas from the Romans, who also had slaves.

In a May 15, 2005 *New York Times* article, "Class in America: Shadowy Lines That Still Divide," the authors say there was a time when American upper crust vacationed in Europe and worshiped an

Episcopal God. The middle class drove Ford Fairlanes, settled the San Fernando Valley and enlisted as company men. The working class belonged to the AFL-CIO, voted Democratic and did not take vacations. Now it's harder to define class, but it's still with us.

I read a book about early Scots-Irish settlers who came here to escape unfair English laws that prevented them from selling their crops to anyone but their overlords. When the Scots-Irish arrived on our shores, particularly in Virginia or Carolina, and were met by English faces, they didn't even spend the night but plunged immediately west into the wilderness west to escape discrimination.

So stratified society began in this country even before we were a nation. In the twentieth century, we held to the belief that with education everyone could move up, and for the generation that came of age during World War II, this seemed to be so. Still, greed abounds, and even government regulations against monopolies and robber barons couldn't stop a few from taking advantage of the many.

Upper mobility is not higher in the U.S. than in Britain or France, even though both countries had hereditary nobilities. It is lower than in Canada and some Scandinavian countries but not as low as in developing countries like Brazil, where escape from poverty is so difficult that the lower class is all but frozen in place.

Those comparisons seem hard to believe. Britain still has a queen. Our founding document proclaimed all men to be created equal. American economy has also grown more quickly than Europe's in recent decades, leaving an impression of boundless opportunity.

But the U.S. differs from Europe in ways that can gum up the mobility machine. Because income inequality is greater here, there is a wider disparity between what rich and poor parents can invest in their children. Perhaps as a result, a child's economic background is a better predictor of school performance in the U.S. than in Denmark, the Netherlands or France, one recent study found.

"Being born in the elite in the U.S. gives you a constellation of privileges that very few people in the world have ever experienced," Berkeley economist David I. Levine says. "Being born poor in the U.S. gives you disadvantages unlike anything in Western Europe and Japan and Canada."

Witness the number of lives lost in New Orleans alone in the aftermath of Hurricane Katrina. With few exceptions, those who were stranded and thus became victims were at the bottom of the economic scale. (One female member of the Spanish Parliament was among those left in the Superdome, but a special helicopter quickly swept in and escorted her out, while thousands around her were left in squalor, trying to survive among dead bodies.)

February 29: * Views on good and evil: Jacobean dramatists Webster, Middleton, Tourneur, and Ford wrote of a treacherous, rotten world characterized by sin unpunished and innocence destroyed. They had a sure grasp of catastrophe. They understood not only evil, but the extravagance of tricks by which evil presents itself as good.

* Hindu saying: "God sleeps in the minerals, awakes in the plants, walks in the animals, and thinks in man."

* Buddhist saying: "Look in the direction you want to go and start walking."

* Jesus said, "Judge not that you be not judged."

* Lao Tzu said, "The good man does not seek culprits; he seeks solutions."

* The difference between boys and girls: When son Andy was about five, I found a deep scratch on the desk. I called to the most likely culprit, playing nearby with a small metal car. "Did you do this?" I asked. Without hesitation, Andy turned those huge blue eyes up to me and said, "Yes, I did it" and stood ready to take his lumps.

I was too stunned to answer. I expected some defense, some excuse, which would have been my own tactic at that age.

Compare that with what happened when daughter Annabeth was five and I discovered a great hunk of her long curls missing. "Did you cut your hair?" I asked. She answered, "Harold made me do it." (Harold was our dog!)

Incidentally, I still have the desk, and the scratch hardly shows. Big to-do over nothing.

March:

March 1: * The roots of Mardi Gras go back to Roman times when March 1 was considered New Year's Day. The Roman Saturnalia was apparently alternately practiced in the spring before March 1, and in the Roman month of December, which was at one time the end of the Roman year. Romans borrowed the customs from ancient Babylon more than 3,500 years before the birth of Christ. During the celebration the rules of order were suspended much like modern-day Mardi Gras celebrations. It was believed that during this time the "god king" descended into the underworld. While he was gone, masters served slaves. A condemned criminal might be paraded through the streets as a sort of Carnival King (an *interrex*, or interim king). Throughout the New Year's month (at the time of the vernal equinox by their calendar) the dead were believed to have returned.

* In Bulgaria, March 1 or the so-called Baba Marta (Grandma Marta) holiday, marks the end of the winter and the beginning of the spring. Bulgarians present relatives and friends with a Martenitsa—a red-and-white woolen thread that is worn fastened either on the clothes or around the wrist- on that very special day. Tradition says that the red color, will protect the people from disease and evil and the white color will make you live longer.

Baba Marta is either severe and cruel, making the whole country white with snow, or mild and kind, giving health and strength through her Martenitsas. Martenitsas are supposed to be worn until the person sees the first stork, then hung onto a tree.

On the first of March, Bulgarians wish each other health and happiness with "Chestita Baba Marta" (in English, "Happy Grandma Marta"). "Marta" comes *Mart*, from the Bulgarian word for March.

March 2: * Early myth and ritual concerning renewal began in ancient Sumer about 3500 B.C.E. Symbolically, in this old vegetation myth, the king died in the winter and was revived when spring arrived. Thus he was crowned every year when he returned. The annual coronation of the king was held in connection with the New Year's festival. In ancient Babylon this was called the *Akitu* ceremony. The Sumerian name *Akitu* means "power making the world live again."

Many scholars believe it was celebrated on the new moon during March, in association with the vernal equinox; however, some report it was apparently celebrated alternately in association with the vernal equinox (Babylonian month of Nisan) or the autumnal equinox (Babylonian month of Tisrit).

The festival, lasting twelve days, combined elements of Mardi Gras (or Halloween), Easter, a joust, coronation and royal wedding. Variations of the ceremony under various names were practiced in Babylon, Assyria, Phoenicia, Canaan and Israel, where they can be found in the book of Psalms.

One version of the great vegetation myth is the Canaanite Epic of Baal, in which the hero Baal decides to challenge the god of death, Mot, by descending to the underworld. His consort Anath, goddess of love and war, grieves for him, and a drought settles over the land. She adorns herself with human skulls and tracks Mot down, cutting him to bits. The great god El, learning that his son Baal is still alive, orders a celebration, and the drought is ended. (This is an abbreviated version. There's a much more detailed account in my *Encyclopedia of Traditional Epics.*)

Unlike other people of the time, the Hebrews declared Baal "evil" and put to death anyone caught worshiping him or any of the other vegetation gods. This intolerance of others' beliefs was the chief cause for attacks on the Jews which have continued into our time.

March 3: * Marion Woodman says you can experience the healing that's going on through observing the love, "a huge energy," she calls it, that exists between two people. She says you can see the light in the other's body and feel it in your own. Of the light, she says that conscious femininity is light in matter, "embodied light, the wisdom of the body." She likens the situation to psychics, where matter moves toward light. By the same token, in the psyche, unconsciousness tends to move toward light. She calls pure spirit "disembodied light." She imagines the androgyne as being soul (embodied light) receiving spirit. That's when creativity happens.

March 4: * My first piano teacher, Virginia Manly Bryan, used to praise me to high heaven and make me think that I could do anything. Sure enough, under her tutelage, I could. When I became a piano teacher, I remembered what miracles Mrs. Bryan wrought with her encouragement, so I treated my students the same way.

A sixth-grade English teacher, Miss James, praised me in the same way and is probably responsible for my having become a writer.

Since I'm aware of the effect that words of encouragement have on me, I use the same positive words to my body. By recognizing love in myself, I try to envision the flow of life constantly restoring me to health. I try to recognize the magic that love brings.

March 5: * The most familiar rites of mortification come in the month of Ramadan for Muslims and the period of Lent for Christians. Ramadan is the last month of the Muslim year, and Lent is actually a year-end period of abstinence—only four hundred years ago the New Year was celebrated on March 1.

* Jim Rosemergy: The desire for something indicates strength. The need for it indicates weakness.

March 6: * To heal someone is to rob him of his *daemon*. At the point when we cave, the point of vulnerability, is actually where the god can enter. The god comes in though the wound; healing *has* to come through the wound. To be human, to be in the body, means to suffer, and suffering is ultimately healing. The message of Christianity is that real love involves immense suffering. Any creative work comes from that level where we love enough to share our suffering, just the sheer suffering of being human.

March 7: * Jung says the opposite of love is not hate, but power. If we have power over someone, we cannot love him/her. Feeling and love are more important than power.

* Some members of the fair sex were not considered important enough for historians to record their names, but their deeds lived on. A case in point was the crusty Turko-Mongol dowager regent whose name did not survive, the widow of A-pao-ki, who died in 926. She supposedly ruled "with" her son but in fact held sole power. Her way of dealing with recalcitrant ministers was to dispatch them to the land of the departed "to take news of her to her late husband." When one wily old Chinese was condemned to such a fate, in his best courtly manner, he suggested that such a high honor should go

to her instead. The empress expressed regrets that, because of obligations to her subjects, she was unable to join her husband, but she would send along a personal token. She called for a sword and lopped off one of her own hands, awarding it to the shaken Chinese diplomat to deliver to her husband in person. Her idea of being fair.

March 8: * So long as we are determined to move at our swift, logical pace, our inner child can't dream. The natural rhythms of the body are slow. If we give ourselves half an hour with our dreams or our music—however our creativity wants to emerge—the soul becomes very quiet. That's why creativity is so healing. In order to be creative, to engage in soul-making, we have to listen to the body. True creativity comes from that deep communication with the archetypal world, where the real nourishment is.

March 9: * The idea of someone swallowing his emotions appears to fit with the cultural notion of the fat person as being complacent and sweet. Often the fat person has decided to perform for the culture. Whatever anyone wants, the fat person will try to please, all the time hating himself for not being truly himself. He may rage inside, and the rage may be against himself for betraying his own needs. The anger concretizes. The fat body is the rebel against the culture's thin ideal.

But the voice that says, "I am lovable" is in the cells. It's at the cellular level that the transformation must take place.

March 10: * I had a frightening dream in which I (we—my husband, or *animus*, and I) were chased by a wild man who had escaped out of the bottom of his cage and was chasing us up a flight of stairs. This morning I understood what my unconscious was trying to convey: I work fairly diligently and seriously for many hours each day. I often neglect my "wilder" nature, which must escape from the "bottom" and is now demanding attention as I try to climb higher and higher. This dream comes as spring is bursting forth, and my spirit apparently wants to cavort with the birds and squirrels and "get down," maybe to dig in the earth.

Two decades ago I duplicated this dream in real life. I married a "wild" man. He even looked wild to me—I was used to very neat, clean-shaven well-disciplined men, and Bill has an unruly beard to match his unruly nature. This beard was and is, to me, the symbol of wildness because it rather breaks the rules. In my circumspect, circumscribed life, this beard is *daring*. It is my attempt to honor the "natural" side of my nature.

This beard represents the same to Bill, who comes from a very disciplined German-Episcopalian family and in reality isn't the least bit wild but is somewhat inhibited. In fact, when he breaks any of his own rules, he hums little short hums that he isn't even aware of.

March 11: * The evilness of the serpent does not appear outside Judaeo-Christian myth. Pliny the Elder (A.D. 23-79), who went to hear the teachings of the Druids, acquired a Druid's Egg—of a serpent which was once kept suspended in the air by the hissing of serpents—which supposedly bestowed great powers on the possessor. A Japanese legend called "The Vision of Hojo-no-Tokimasa" tells of a maiden who prays fervently for three weeks to the goddess Benzaitan for protection. After that time, Tokimasa is granted a dream/vision of Benzaitan who appears to her in the form of a serpent. As she disappears, Benzaitan leaves behind three scales as a pledge of divine protection.

* Likewise, the evil associated in our society with the term "crone," which seems to connote "witch" to us, doesn't appear in other cultures. Our fear of aging makes the crone into an image of evil and prevents us from accepting this archetype as a source of new creative power. We can't let ourselves realize that the Old Woman or Hag carries the key to success.

* New energies come into conscious awareness through violent occurrences that involve severe loss.

In mythology, the crone is the archetypal wise old woman. As the "thousand-named goddess," she is known as Tiamat, the birth-giving ocean; Maat, the white feather of truth; Medusa, whose countenance could turn men into stone; Fata Morgana, who brought men to their fate; Sophia, highest wisdom; Hecate, goddess of crossroads; Brigit, who brought the cycles of the seasons; Kali, who destroyed so that creation could come into being; Syrian Mari, who could search the soul; Kuan Yin, the Buddhist manifestation of Great Love and Great Compassion, whose name means "she who hears the cries of the world" and in one aspect is Universal Mother; Baba Yaga, the dark one or the witch: a terror unto to those who reject or try to manipulate her; and many more.

This last, Baba Yaga, dwells in her hut in the woods of the unconscious, cut off from the conscious world of daily life. Even her name calls up images of an old hag who fattens up children before she eats them. The dark crone has also been known as the harbinger of illness of death or worse, senility. Sometimes she brings the psychological death of an old way of being.

It's true we must free ourselves from the devouring mother who kills the values of consciousness, but not by killing her: in the eyes of nature, matricide is the unforgivable crime. Real freedom from this dark archetype must come through acceptance of the furies of instinct without losing conscious values, thus redeeming them.

(The Furies were those terrible goddesses whose hair was writhing snakes, whose chief characteristic is instinctual revenge. They are instinctual creatures, but their name, the Eumenides, ironically means "the kindly ones." Their story is told in Aeschylus' play, *The Eumenides*. Aeschylus calls them "the ancient children," for they are ruthless, but also have the spontaneous vitality of the child. We reject this part of our nature at our own peril.)

As Hecate/Demeter/Persephone, she is the gatekeeper at the doors of birth and death. Her eider priestesses are *dakinis*, "sky walkers," who prepare the dying for their transition and lead them in spirit form into the mysterious "Land of the Intermediate State." We recognize in this term echoes of the later Catholic tradition of Purgatory. As the agent of change, she is the "Earth-Shaker" who comes out of her cave and shakes her rain stick to alter the world.

She is also, in Longfellow's words, "Nature, the old nurse," who takes the child upon her knee and teaches secrets of the universe.

Demeter is mother goddess, producer of all beings, earth mother, corn mother, guardian of birth and fruitfulness. As triple goddess, Demeter's myth reaches out to us wherever we are in our life span. If we see her as maiden, the Kore, she shows her youthfulness. As mother, she shows nurturing. As crone, we see her as Hecate, ancient one of the crossroads. If we look at all three in terms of the liminal years before old age, we can see that all three are one.

As wise woman and keeper of the cauldron, the crone knows

the secret of regeneration. The word crone itself is related to *crown,* and in tribal societies, she represents the power of the matriarch who makes the moral and legal decisions for her subjects and descendants. In certain African cultures such as Ashanti, she still chooses the next ruler. As the embodiment of wisdom, she is supposed to have written the first tablets of law and punished the first sinners.

Once the crone has been introduced into our consciousness, she is not going to leave us alone. She seeks creative form, and if she is squelched, she may become destructive, causing all sorts of havoc until she is given space in our lives.

Demeter's doorway is that place under the lintel between two worlds: the one in which our sun shines, and the other which is before and outside creation, where all things have their source.

March 12: * The healer is always an "intercessor," not a remover of symptoms, which only go from one place to another. Interceding by his/her own experience of suffering, the healer, the Christ, carries for the other, as the other carries for him. "Intercede" is kin to the word "forgive" or "pardon." To "give for" is an expression of the love that "endures all things, bears all things."

Sometimes what the healer brings is a new version of the "facts": a new vision of the way things are. We often hold untested beliefs as private certainties. Our analytic model claims universal validity instead of realizing its contingent status. What we see as "reality" is inseparable from our language and our activities.

David Bohm says: "The ability to perceive or think differently is more important than the knowledge gained."

Cognition isn't a representation of the world "out there" but rather a bringing forth of the world by the process of living. As humans, the only world we can have is the one we create together through our interactions and our language. Our world will change only if *we* change. The healer is one who can help us realize this.

March 13: * Since the time of Teddy Roosevelt every president has brought more public lands under the protection of the federal government—until Geroge W. Bush. He has weakened protections on 234 million acres, an area roughly equal to Texas plus Oklahoma, all in the interest of making more land available for oil exploration.

(What became of his plan to encourage development of the electric car?) Before his era, we had a Roadless Area Conservation Rule, which protected almost 60 million acres of national forests and thus also gave precious wildlife a place of sanctuary.

There's a biblical word, "dominion," which is not the same as "domination." If we don't preserve our treees and our wildlife for future generations, what will be left for them?

March 14: * To alter our reality requires sacrifice and suffering, insofar as every liberation is linked to a prohibition by the conservative superego. But if we succeed in tolerating our sense of guilt for having broken this potent law, we also succeed in grasping the creative value of our act of separation and detachment from a past that immobilizes us.

March 15: * In mythology, a theft is always an act of courage. It has to do with making our own future, not being boxed in by the roles family or society has given us to play.

* In Lakota society, the morning begins with prayer. The medicine man burns a bit of sage of sweet grass—a practice called "smudging." He acknowledges or calls to the powers of the Four Directions, to Father Sky and to Mother Earth. Then he prays to God. During the day, parents, including aunts and uncles, teach the next generation practical skills: how to sew, how to make tools, how to procure food. Grandparents and other elders teach about life: spirituality and character. Humility, compassion, and selflessness are the three core values of the Lakota. The process of instilling these values involves simple instruction and story-telling.

One story involves Crazy Horse, who defeated General George Custer at the Battle of Big Horn. Crazy Horse's boyhood name was Light Hair, who grew up learning the virtues of a *wica*, or "complete man," entrusted to provide for and protect his family and community. Sitting Bull, Red Cloud, and Spotted Tail were three of the influential figures in his life. As a young man, Crazy Horse's selfless actions and skill beyond his years earned him the title of "shirt wearer," who is esteemed but challenged to live a life beyond reproach.

March 16: * We often remain silent for fear that to speak would mean to alienate other people's love and draw derision upon ourselves. The childish fear of being abandoned remains with us into adulthood. We observe it in people who have an extreme need always to be surrounded by friends and who do their utmost to keep parental ties alive, even to the extent of agreeing with their opinions. Such persons become banal, because to say anything new, they would have to undergo conflicts. Aeschylus says that few men are capable of loving without envying a friend who has experienced good fortune. Successful people must learn to recognize and deal with envy.

Anyone who has something new to say must pay the price of ostracism and prepare to be subject to the law: no one is a prophet in his own country. But we should also realize whenever we try anything new that what paralyzes us is our own fear. The struggle to assert and express oneself is never primarily external. There are people who become blocked even when they have to write a friendly letter, because they're afraid of exposing themselves at any level.

Everyone who sets out on the road of his own destiny must reckon with the envy of others. Often society, even his own family, makes him the scapegoat, or the black sheep.

Sometimes it works the other way. The one who remains behind, who never tries his wings, who settles for functioning within the parameters set out by the last generation, often blames his inability to act on his own on an external object or circumstance, which has the function of scapegoat. This is singled out as the origin of his misfortune at never having fulfilled his dreams. It frees the individual from the unpleasant task of facing up to himself, of admitting that the reason he never tried is that he fears rejection, fears failure.

March 17: * The importance of language as an incredible primordial force cannot be over emphasized. We don't use language to *describe* the world; rather, we use it to *create* the world. We don't describe the world we see; we see the world we describe. *So all life is enchanted, and we live in a fantastic universe.*

There are two qualities that make our ability to create so. First is the universe's openness: Physicists have shown that the notion that the world is made up of separate "things" is an illusion. So the truth is that all matter is constantly in motion and is insubstantial. The second quality is the emergent nature of the universe: A group of simple interacting components can suddenly act together *like a band without a leader* to give rise to something new with completely new and different qualities from the components. This can be so because a different "reality" (one of billions of possibilities) is already in the system ready to be brought forth.

This *enchanted universe* was explained by physicist David Bohm as "implicate order," whereby everything is enfolded in everything. In other words, matter has its existence in the whole and manifests in a localized way. If all the "givens" we've always taken for granted are not so—and science has blown great holes in most of these—then huge possibilities are available. If the system is open, constantly fluctuating, we can take a stand and make a declaration to create a new reality for ourselves. If we can arrive at a state of "surrender" to the ground of being that is not controlled by things or instincts, we alter our relationship to the future.

We construct the environment of our enchanted world by our language. *We exist in language, and we only see what we talk about.* Language is like another set of eyes and hands. We lay down a path for knowing the world by an accumulation of recurrent human footprints traveling over the same ground. When we come to realize the truth about our open nature, we communicate this truth through language, and we attract others who are drawn to authenticity. *We recognize the truth when we hear it.* The more people who are drawn into this circle (linked together in meaning" as Martin Buber said about freedom and destiny), the more the group functions like the "interacting components" mentioned above, and a new "third thing" will ultimately develop. This isn't spooky; it is nature's way.

* There's another fundamental about language—including pictures, an earlier form of language. Sometimes we get caught up in "self-help" books which don't seem to help our problem. We read the same message in book after book, but we don't assimilate it. That's because the unconscious understands only *images*, and to make something our own at the gut level, to internalize it, it must be given form: we need to *take action*: to write about it, paint a picture about it, sing about it. Then we have made the message ours.

Maybe, in fact, the author of the self-help book had not made the message his own until he had written it down in a book. Writing the book was his avenue to communicating with his own self.

March 18: * Children and primitive people are wiser than we ever knew. They see life in everything. Superstitious fundamentalists call this paganism. Scientists call it truth. Bell's theorem sees the world as fundamentally connected. At some level we cannot see, there is unbroken wholeness—an order out of which seemingly discrete events arise. All humans are part of that unbroken whole which is continually unfolding from and making itself manifest in the explicate world. We can actually create an opening to the unbroken whole by paying attention to the implicate order that is unfolding. We can create dreams, visions and stories that we sense "want" to happen (as Martin Buber said, "want to be actualized"). By creating scenarios we can help sense and actualize emerging new realities by providing a story.

Leadership is about creating a domain in which we continually learn and become more capable of participating in our unfolding future. A leader sets the stage on which predictable "miracles," or synchronicities, can occur.

But our mental model of the way the world works must shift from the mechanistic, clockwork universe to one more like a child sees things: relationship is the organizing principle of the universe, which is open, dynamic, interconnected, and full of living qualities.

Bohm describes matter as sometimes particles, sometimes waves, sometimes mass, sometimes energy, all interconnected and constantly in motion. Physicist Henry Sapp describes elementary particles as "in essence, a set of relationships that reach outward to other things."

Management theorist Margaret Wheatley says particles come into being ephemerally, through interaction with other energy sources, which are "intermediate states in a network of interactions."

Since the future isn't fixed, we shift from resignation to an attitude of possibility. At every moment we create the future.

* Jonas Salk, developer of the polio vaccine, also spoke of a universe that unfolds kaleidoscopically according to a deeply ingrained order. He believed that people could develop the capacity to tap into this continually unfolding "dynamism"; that people can sense the way the future wants to unfold and can "hurry it along."

He said, "I have come to recognize evolution not only as an active process that I am experiencing all the time, but as something I can guide by the choices I make…." (*New York Times*, 24 June

1993, pp. 1, 9). The child believes this implicitly.

Watch a solitary child at play. She has an attitude of openness. If we want to take advantage of what we've been told is true about the nature of things, we need to develop a commitment to listen to our inner voice, to remain in a state of surrender and trust in the playing out of our own destiny. When we reach this state of surrender, we alter our relationship with the future. We see ourselves as an essential part of the unfolding universe. Our life becomes infused with meaning. Then, like the child, we aren't surprised when doors open and a sense of flow develops. (Emerson speaks of these doors.) Seemingly accidental "coincidences" occur that, if we are paying attention, point us in the right direction.

The child knows she is not alone. How can we operate more consistently with the awareness that we aren't alone in this world? When our way of being shifts, our sense of identity shifts, and we can see ourselves as connected to one another and to the whole universe. In this state, we accept others as legitimate beings, *no matter what their religion, race, gender, or national origin.*

March 19: * We need a language that brings us together about the deepest things we care about. One word that describes the radiance of the Divine that is beyond understanding or description is "numinous."

We often presume that words are the measure. But it is precisely the immeasurable that we care most deeply about: the indefinable, intangible, inexpressible, the real. The western word "measure" and the Sanskrit *maya* have the same root. *Maya* is the most ancient word for "illusion." The prevailing philosophy of the East is that the immeasurable is the primary reality. The entire structure and order of forms that present themselves in ordinary perception are regarded as a sort of veil that covers the true reality which can't be perceived by the senses and about which nothing can be said or thought. (I don't mind not understanding everything.)

March 20: * There are two broad approaches to meeting the day. One is to look on life as something to *escape* by various paths (like watching TV, shopping, eating, taking drugs, yakking with friends)—of living as a burden, in other words—with the self as an isolated being who has to endure the torment of inner demons, or madnesses. (Plato described four divine madnesses: Apollo's prophetic madness, telestic or ritual madness, the poetic madness inspired by the Muses, and the erotic madness of Eros and Aphrodite.)

Two of these Greek gods represent opposite traits. Apollo is, among other things, the god of healing, music, prophecy and light. As Apollo Lykeios, he was also connected with the Lyceum, the teaching place of Aristotle. Dionysus is the god of wine and ecstasy: the giver of joy. He led his followers to throw off their inhibitions and be unafraid to explore the dark. So in a sense, the two could represent order and chaos; civilization and barbarity; law and anarchy; "good" and "evil." The nihilism of our society leads us to the tendency of thinking only in terms of black and white.

That's one way to meet the day. The other is to look upon life as filled with possibilities, choices to make; and not to get too hung up on making judgments about other people's motives, of characterizing everything as either black or white; and to remember that there are layers and layers to our history. (In early days of the Christian era, some pagan mystery cults related Jesus to Orpheus or Dionysus. A recent excavation of the grotto of a mystery cult unearthed a mosaic depicting grapes and bearing the inscription "Jesus Dionysus.")

To simplify: There are two ways to meet the day: thinking about ourselves or thinking about others.

March 21: * A little known fact that so far we've lived without: Tartans and bagpipes both originated outside of Scotland, in Uganda, a country of which Idi Amin once had himself crowned king.

* The penalty for masturbation in Indonesia is decapitation.

* There are men in Guam whose full-time job is to travel the countryside and deflower young virgins, who pay them for the privilege of having sex for the first time...Reason: under Guam law, it is expressly forbidden for virgins to marry.

* In Santa Cruz, Bolivia, it is illegal for a man to have sex with a woman and her daughter at the same time.

March 22: * The Yoruba of West Africa say that certain people are gifted with a unique power called à*she.* They are believed to embody the supernatural powers possessed by certain deities. This trait can manifest itself in leadership qualities, spiritual insight, or creativity. A work of art containing this quality is divine force incarnate. This same quality can be the "power to make things happen" or it can be a morally neutral force that can destroy as well.

In Yoruba myth, there is a deity named Atunda, slave of the powerful god Orisanla. In the beginning, Orisanla possessed all knowledge, truth and consciousness. One day, while Orisanla was sleeping at the bottom of a hill, Atunda, out of envy, rolled a huge rock downhill, shattering Orisanla into millions of bits. Each broken piece became a new deity, one aspect of the whole.

Nobel novelist Wole Soyinka, a Yoruba, has modeled his life after Ogun, the god of iron, the artist-toolmaker-warrior deity who through sheer force of will clears the road by which knowledge reaches the human world.

March 23: * Thomas Mann said, "...[I]s man's ego a thing imprisoned in itself and sternly shut up in its boundaries of flesh and time? Do not many elements which make it up belong to a world before it and outside of it?"

* Freud said the ego is not even master in its own house, but "must content itself with scanty information of what is going on unconsciously in its mind." The "dethroning" of the ego occurs through the emergence of other forces normally held at bay by defense mechanisms.

* Jung said that if one interprets a fairy tale thoroughly, one must take at least a week's holiday afterward, because it is so difficult.

March 24: * A feature of vegetation cultures around the world depicted in the most ancient documents and stele is that the king must die; either he has to be killed or deposed, just as crops die in the winter. He has to be put into the ground, to visit the underworld. Then he goes through a renewal and returns, just as new crops appear in the spring. The story of the life of Jesus follows this pattern, too.

* Collective symbols of the Self wear out; become stale. Religions, convictions, truths, all age. Everything that has been talked about too much and which has for a while ruled human society, ages and becomes impotent, mechanical, too well known, a possession of consciousness. It needs to die and be reborn.

* On March 24, 1603, after weeks of heavy rain, the River Tweed overflowed its banks and for the first time, merged with the waters of Powsail Burn, above which Drumelzier stood. A churchyard in Drumelzier is where Merlin the Wizard was said to be buried. On that same day, Queen Elizabeth I of England died, and James VI of Scotland became also James I of England.

March 25: * The way of girls is different from boys, who tend to fight aggressively to form hierarchies. Girls evince their aggression by maliciously playing tricks or whispering against each other. There is still a jockeying for power, but it's played with a weapon of poison, not with brutality. It's done with needling and little jealousies. Too much of one or the other is detrimental. They are two complementary worlds meant to belong together where their tendency to rule is neutralized. Or ought to be.

The female with a sense of her power among males who is tempted to "betray" a female friend to the males—use her poison, in other words—may recant later when she realizes her need for female friends. But "poison" is an appropriate term. Trust has been permanently poisoned. Her power among other females is diminished. This is not an abstract psychological concept; I've witnessed it.

March 26: * Abandonment is an element that accompanies alcoholism, so alcoholism is a love problem. The alcoholic finds a community in AA and there can get over his feeling, real or imagined, of abandonment. This is Marion Woodman's estimation. Having suffered anorexia, she understands its similarity to alcoholism.

* Addiction in general is a longing for an ecstatic religious state, and yet, practicing alcoholics have blocked their own emotions. They don't have a clue what they are feeling. The drug has seen to that.My own idea is that people try to avoid coming to terms with their own mortality. Some do it inventing religions. Some escape reality by using drugs, alcohol—even gambling or sex.

March 27: * Prior to the fourth century, the concept of Mary's virginity was unknown to Catholicism. Then suddenly the physical virginity of Mary became important to the leaders of the church. Ambrose, on reading Ezekiel 44: 1-3, saw a prophetic indication of this virgin birth: "What is this gate if not Mary? ... through which Christ entered this world when he came forth from a virginal birth and did break the closed genitals of virginity."

There were sects that believed that the Holy Ghost was feminine, and therefore a holy family of father, mother and son dwelled in Heaven. But these beliefs were repressed by the church councils, which decided that the Holy Ghost was masculine.

At the Council of Ephesus in 431, Mary was declared to be Theotokos, Mother of God. Her cult spread like wildfire, helped along by Justinian, Narses, John of Samascus, Peter Damian. Following the first change came the dogma of the Immaculate Conception, then the newest dogma of the Assumption. Although the Assumption has been generally believed since about the eleventh century, it was only finally confirmed in 1950 by Pope Pius XII.

After the Pope declared the Assumption of the Virgin, many priests wanted to marry, and nuns wanted to become priestesses. Why did they suddenly want to marry or to be priestesses? Psychologists believe it is the archetype of the feminine rising in the collective unconscious: surface waves from something happening deep in the ocean of the collective unconscious. The feminine image wants to surface. This is a build-up beginning with ancient times.

Much of early Christian iconography came from earlier models. Angels in picture or sculpture were borrowed from statues of Nike, Goddess of Victory. On early Christian coffins, the winged beings depicted giving a crown to the dead person is copied from the schema of Nike bestowing crowns to contestants in the Olympian Games.

The Virgin Mary's earliest uncovered depiction is a copy of the Egyptian goddess Isis and her child Horus. Isis is the Great Mother, and also the Mother of God, the new Sun God Horus, and wife of the reborn Osiris. In the Late Roman Empire, Isis played a very large role. She inherited or attracted to herself traits of many other Mediterranean mother goddesses, like Derceto-Atargatis and Anat. The Isis mysteries were linked to the Mithraic mysteries: there are many Mithraic sanctuaries bearing both Mithra and Isis iconography.

Although Isis represented the highest divine, she was also worshipped as goddess of the underworld, ruler of the dead, of ghosts, and night. She was a black goddess, not only in the sense of evil, but also in the sense of nocturnal, earthy. In the late Egyptian tradition, she was also mixed with Sekmet, the lion goddess, and Bastet, cat goddess. Virgin Mary inherited traits of Isis, but the official Church never fully recognized the traits beyond purity, such as earth fertility.

However, among the peasant population in agricultural cultures, all those traits not recognized by Church dogma are alive and well in the worship of Mary. For example, in Latin America there is the Madonna of Guadeloupe, who has clearly inherited all the attributes of the Indian mother fertility goddess.

March 28: * Apples have a long history of possessing special qualities. Although the biblical Tree of Knowledge of Good and Evil wasn't specifically called an apple tree, Christian mythology has made it so. Eve stole an apple and thereby brought to mankind the possibility of consciousness and the certainty of death. So the apple has come to symbolize the conveying of consciousness.

Another apple tree is the one bearing the Golden Apples of the Hesperides, which also had to be stolen. The Hesperides lie west of Greece, toward the setting sun, the direction of death and of entry into the unconscious. In some versions, the tree was given to Hera (Zeus's wife) by Mother Earth (Gaia) as a wedding present. Getting the Golden Apples was Hercules' eleventh labor and the only one where he had to use his wits instead of his strength. He had to outwit Atlas to get them.

When Eris, goddess of discord and strife, was not invited to a wedding on Olympus, she threw a golden apple labeled, "For the fairest." Zeus refused to decide whether it should go to Hera, Athena or Aphrodite, and he passed the job to Paris, Priam's son. Hera offered him power if he chose her; Athena offered him military victory; Aphrodite offered him the most beautiful women in the world. He chose Aphrodite, who then helped him steal Menelaus' wife Helen (Helen of Troy), causing the Trojan War. All started by an apple.

In Norse mythology Iduna has golden apples that rejuvenate the gods, keep them youthful, and thus confer eternal life.

Avalon, the island of apples, is where King Arthur goes at the end of his life.

March 29: * In our culture there are mysteries and possible archetypal, inner realizations connected with childbirth, which many women miss out on. Psychologist Marie-Louise Von Franz believes this is due to the patriarchal tradition and to the fact that the image of woman is robbed of her biological, natural under half. I missed out on the birth of my first child, because I was drugged. Even for the births of my other children I wasn't fully aware of the depth of the mystery. This didn't strike me at the gut level until I assisted my daughter in her first labor. It was such a deep, mystical experience, it literally changed the course of my life. I felt a connection to the earth I'd never felt before. I made some drastic decisions as a result —or rather, the experience somehow made the decisions for me.

March 30: * Dogs have been man's companions since cavemen times, but cats were being promoted to divinity in early Egypt, where cats originated. The cat was considered sacred to Isis. It is still considered beneficent in Egypt. As the daughter of Isis and Osiris, the great cat goddess Bastet emerged in the twenty-second dynasty and took precedence over all other goddesses. Bastet has to do with fertility, with folk festivals, and also with music. The sistrum, the musical instrument of Isis, is often depicted with cats in ancient excavations. She was known as the Lady of Bubastis. Her temple stood at the center of the city, surrounded by water.

At Bastet's festival, people went down the Nile on barges, and the women lifted their skirts and "mooned" the people on the shore, who applauded and cheered! Fertility, sexual rites, even lasciviousness were part of the fun.

The gods Osiris, Ra and Horus often merge in Egyptian myth. Bastet, the sun cat, was often indentified with her father, Ra, the god of life. It was believed that every night she struggled with Apophis, the serpent of darkness. The cat was also worshipped as lunar. During nighttime, the sun's rays were reflected in the cat's phosphorescent eyes, as sun's light is reflected by the moon.

During the late period in Egypt, Bastet was identified with the Greek hunting goddess Artemis, virgin goddess of nature, fertility, childbirth. One story tells that Typhon chased the Greek gods to Egypt, where Artemis transformed into a cat and hid in the moon.

Hecate also turned herself into a cat. With the Teutonic fertility goddess Freya, who was married to the sun and whose carriage was pulled by two cats, Hecate also represents the Terrible Mother, the witch, responsible for madness.

The whole devilish aspect of the cat has come to the forefront with the Christian era. That has to do with the patriarchal banishing of the feminine shadow.

This dark side, the black cat, practiced orgies on moonless nights. Intercourse with the devil, who often took the form of a cat, produced hail, storms, destruction of crops, death of animals, and impotence in humans. The black cat poisoned people's minds, infected their bodies with disease and inflicted blindness on them. The black cat is an omen of bad luck. Its eyes could paralyze its victims. The devil used his cat tail to bewitch people.

Conversely, the white cat was a seer, healer and nurse who strengthened people's recuperation, and the white cat's tail was used to cure blindness. In fairy tales, the white cat aids the poor and uses its cunning to combat the powers of darkness. It also brings wealth, power, and honor. The solar cat can be seen at the foot of Christ, while the demon cat sits at the foot of Judas.

In the Middle Ages, the cat was embued with the power of the devil, and some women (witches) were said to be able to put their souls into black cats. We have Catholic dissociation from sexuality and instincts in general to thank for satanizing the cat, which in Egypt was linked to fertility through Bastet's sexual orgies.

According to Gnostic belief, there was a cat in the Garden of Eden, guarding the tree of life with its knowledge of good and evil. In Egyptian myth, the solar cat was associated with the Persea tree, a tree of life and consciousness.

A Celtic myth tells how an oracular shrine was found in a cave. Inside, a sleek cat lay on a silver couch. The cat was thus a mediam, forming a bridge between good and evil, with knowledge of both. Wisdom was attributed to the cat. It has uncanny qualities of balance, and it can teach us about balance of various kinds in our lives.

March 31: * On Good Friday, Jesus Christ hung on the tree, as Wotan before him hung on Yggdrasil, the spinning axle of the world, as did Attis and Marsyas of antiquity. The human race has a penchant for crucifying its saviors on trees.

* According to Reis Inc., a commercial real estate market research company, in the 1980s, the average size of an office cubicle

was 227 square feet. In 2004, cubicle size had shrunk to 150 from 200 square feet. Remember when people used to have offices?

* A fox guarding the henhouse story: Philip A Cooney, a White House official who once led the oil industry's fight against limits on greenhouse gases, has repeatedly *edited government climate reports* in ways that play down links between such emissions and global warming, according to internal documents.

In handwritten notes on drafts of several reports issued in 2002 and 2003, Cooney, *removed* or "adjusted" descriptions of climate research that government scientists and their supervisors, including some senior Bush administration officials had already approved.

The dozens of changes, while sometimes as subtle as the insertion of the phrase "significant and fundamental" before the word "uncertainties," tend to produce an air of doubt about findings that most climate experts say are robust.

Mr. Cooney is chief of staff for the White House Council on Environmental Quality, that helps devise and promote administration policies on environmental issues. A good old crony.

* Dr. Carl Jung had these words carved over the door of his house in Zurich: "*VOCATVS atoue non VOCATVS Deus aderit*". The meaning is: "Bidden or not bidden, God is present."

After his death, the same words were inscribed on his tombstone.

* Tom Harper, writing for *The Toronto Star,* and repeated in the *Times Literary Supplement* (London), reported on a conference at the Village Baptist Church in Destin, Alabama:

"I have never heard so much venom and dangerous ignorance spouted before an utterly unquestioning, otherwise normal-looking crowd in my life.... There were stunning statements about humans having been only 6,000 years on Earth and other denials of contemporary geology and biology. And we learned that the Rapture, which could happen any second now, but certainly withing the next 40 years, will instantly sweep all the 'saved' Americans (perhaps one-half the population) to heaven...."

The speakers: Tim LaHaye and Jerry B. Jenkins.

April

April 1: * In Zen Buddhism's famous series of the Ten Ox-herding Pictures there is finally the picture of *satori* (enlightenment), which is the image of the old man with a beggar's bowl going about the market. The description says: "He has forgotten the gods, he has forgotten enlightenment, he has forgotten everything, but wherever he walks, the cherry tree blossoms."

This reminds me of a story told by Rabbi Kahn about a rabbi who asks a pupil: "Which is more to be desired: to be a nonbeliever but to continue to pray, or to be a believer and not pray?" The answer is, surprisingly, to be a nonbeliever but continue to pray, the reasoning being that eventually prayer works anyway.

April 2: * April 2 is the traditional April Fools' Day in the Orkney Islands. It's called Tailing Day, when "tails" or rude messages are pinned on people's backs in honor of the Celtic god Lud, god, among other things, of humor. Lud seems to have been holding sway on the Orkneys for quite some time. Early in the eighteenth century, a woman in Stromness made her living selling winds to the mariners. They cost sixpence each, which was pretty high at that time.

April 3: * In April of 1917, America entered World War I, called the Great War, until World War II came along. I had several older uncles on both sides of the family who served in that conflict, and all lived to tell about it—although they seldom did.

The Great War began in August of 1914, in response to the June murder of the heir to the throne of Austria-Hungary, Archduke Franz Ferdinand, by a Serbian nationalist. (Serbian unrest has been going on since before the Battle of Kosovo in the 1400's. The more recent Bosnian War is another of many attempts by outsiders to subdue a people who want to be independent.) Originally Austria-Hungary and Germany, the Central Powers, went to war against Great Britain, France, and Russia, called the Allies. Then Bulgaria and the Ottoman Empire (Turkey, et. al.) joined the Central Powers, and eventually Japan and Italy, among others, joined the Allies.

President Woodrow Wilson ran for re-election in 1916 on the

slogan, "He Kept Us Out of War." But after German submarines sank U.S. ships, and Britain uncovered a German plot to turn Mexico against the U.S., we changed our minds about wanting to remain neutral. About the time we entered the war, the Bolsheviks, who had taken over Russia, made a separate peace with the Central Powers and were no longer among the Allies.

April 4: * Psychoanalyst Marion Woodman says that intuitive people are never quite in their bodies. "They are rarely in the present, never filling their bodies, which therefore become vulnerable to all the pain in their environment...." Among intuitives, the soul is hiding somewhere in the gut; it isn't animating the whole body. "You feel that when addicts hug you...," she says. Alone, we dialogue with our own bodies, our souls, whose wisdom is exactly what we need for our own wholeness. It makes clear what is real, what is illusion. It strips off layers of false pride. It makes us human.

April 5: * Among the Hottentots, the initiation of a boy into adult life provides for the son's ritual union with his mother, because it is through the active possession of the mother herself that the necessary detachment from the child's world takes place.

April 6: * In tribal cultures old people are the guardians of life's mysteries and the laws. They are the storytellers who pass on songs and sagas of age-old traditions, the sacred or totemic aspect of culture, giving context to the tribe.

The shaman, often a man crippled or wounded from birth, had special powers to enter the spirit world and bring back messages of wisdom to the tribe from various gods. Therefore, he was traditionally also the healer, the savior. The priest was a latter day incarnation of the shaman. He spoke in a mysterious tongue the congregants couldn't understand. He alone had the power to give the messages—even the body—of the deity to the worshippers. The wounded healer is a savior figure in many cultures.

* Almost immediately the concept of one God wasn't sufficient in our small minds to embody all the aspects that people intuited a deity had. The one God became three: the Trinity. But soon the pull of ancient wisdom demanded that even more aspects of the godhead

be personified, and so saints were added. Many people rejected this concept, and some turned to science as the new god. The mystery is an extremely complicated concept, one too great for us to wrap our minds around. So the shaman and the tribal elders may be as near to the core of things as their twenty-first century counterparts.

April 7: * One more bit of information I wonder how I ever lived without: Sometime along about now each year, Good Friday comes. In Great Britain, and in Episcopalian Northeastern U.S., hot cross buns are traditional fare. This custom actually began in pre-Christian times, however, when the god Zeus was given a bun decorated with a cross, which represented oxen horns.

April 8: * During the Nazi period, the Nuremberg Law decreed that Jews were an inferior race. In the face of the law's absurdity, the Aryans didn't protest but hurled themselves like hyenas upon the Jews, confiscating their property, depriving them of their professions, their livelihood, their humanity. It was the *law* that allowed them to do it. Even the 1905 Nobel physicist Philipp Lenard tried to discredit Albert Einstein's work on the basis of the fact that he was a Jew. And nobody played Mendelssohn's music in Germany.

My friend Inge spent part of her childhood in a work camp because her father was part Jew. She sat in a room with a pile of feathers which she stripped by hand for down to make pillows. Her hands were constantly raw and bleeding. Her father remained in hiding all during World War II, sometimes appearing at their home at night when the grown-ups thought the children were asleep.

Later Inge was placed in a different work camp, where they were awakened very early each morning and marched to a factory several miles away. One morning no one came to wake them. The camp was silent. They went outside and found the gates open, and no sign of Nazi guards. Soon the Americans appeared, and there was general rejoicing.

Inge lost her mother and baby brother during the war, but after the war, some Yanks gave Inge a jeep ride to the home of her uncle, where she was sure her father had been hiding. When she knocked on the door, he opened it. He was so emaciated that he had to hold his trousers up with one hand. When he saw his daughter, he threw open his arms—and lost his pants! They were both able to laugh about it, at a time when they had so much to cry about.

April 9: * Marion Woodman, who has worked with addicts, says alcoholism is about losing a connection with the spirit, and grabbing a surrogate spirit of some kind. In late stages of drinking, she says, men become effeminate, full of resentments, complaining, making whiney, poisonous remarks. They are at the mercy of their moods. When they are not drinking they are depressed and resentful. They drink because nobody loves them. It's unclear whether the deterioration of the *anima* (soul, or spirit) causes the drinking or is caused by the drinking, but either way, she says, they go together.

* We now know that we and gorillas share 98% of the same genes. We know that our primitive, or reptilian, brain houses our instincts. What makes us different is the huge frontal lobes of our brain. I read an article by Dr. Ben Carson, the neurosurgeon responsible for the 23-hour operation separating the Binder Siamese twins from Germany. He said that by placing elecrtodes into the parts of the human brain that control memory and stimulating it, an 85-year-old could quote verbatim a newspaper article s/he had read a half century earlier. It is a three-pound powerhouse. But what Dr. Carson came to realize is that the human brain is simply a mechanical component of an entity of far greater beauty and power: the mind.

April 10: * Linen has healing power in Ireland, where particular remedies have to be wrapped in pure linen before using. You pass linen over warts or some diseased spot of the body, then put the linen into a coffin.

Among the Czechs, the newborn child is wrapped in linen and then put under the table so that it will be intelligent.

In northern Germany, one takes white linen to bed to look into the future on New Year's night. Dreams of white things, like linen, point to death. In Brandenburg, a newborn has to be wrapped in pure linen because otherwise, later, it might run after the other sex.

In Romanian tradition, a dream of linen refers to a journey wherein it is important whether the linen is spread out or rolled up.

April 11: * The unconscious fantasies of people are their destiny.

A Russian fairy tale tells of the three sons of the Tsar who go out riding and come to a sign that says, "He who rides to the right side will remain hungry, but his horse will have enough to eat. He who goes to the left will have enough to eat, but his horse will go hungry. He who goes straight ahead will suffer death." The eldest goes to the right and brings a copper snake back to his father, who chases him away. The second son goes to the left and ends up in a brothel, where he is caught by a prostitute and never goes home again. The youngest, who rides straight ahead, goes through terrible trials and ordeals, where he appears to be dead. But finally he revives and returns home to become Tsar.

To go right means to follow consciousness. The eldest brother chooses a materialistic way. He sees that he has money and health and that his horse is well fed. His body, his physical being, is also well fed. But he starves his spiritual side.

The second brother has something to eat, but his horse gets nothing. He thinks the important things are spiritual values and human relationships, and neglects his physical and material needs.

The youngest, who goes the middle way, remains between the opposites and thus is able to use all parts of his nature and survive any ordeal. He is the one who is fit to rule.

April 12: * The Greeks interpret rain as a loving embrace of Zeus and Demeter, the sky god and the earth. In the *I Ching*, there are many oracles that say such things as "When the rain falls, good luck comes." Literally, when the rain falls, there is a solution. Thus, a thunderstorm is a clash of opposites that leads to a solution.

April 13: * The general meaning everywhere of ringing bells is to keep demons away. The devil hates the ringing of a bell. In the Catholic Mass it marks a transition point when the transubstantiation is immanent. The bell unites the opposites. It's a symbol for totality because it unites the clapper (masculine) and the bell (feminine). The bell rings and it is the moment of eternity, when something important is happening.

* Clocks sometimes have "magical" aspects. Many people have a connection with their clocks, so when they die, the clock ceases to work. Or something archetypal or very important happens and their

watch stops at that precise moment. Jung described such a infinity or eternity coming into clock time. Eternity interrupts. It is as if there is a plane where there is clock time and then eternity puts its hand in for a minute and one has an archetypal experience.

April 14: * Christian and Muslim who have despised the flesh have to realize, says Marie-Louise Von Franz, that the flesh is a form of the divine, a divine revelation, and that sexuality is something divine.

* The word "metaphor" is from the Greek *meta*, "over, across," plus *pherein,* "to carry." A written metaphor carries one across from a happening to its meaning. So does an image, such as might appear in dreams.

* The word "analysis" is from the Greek *analusis,* meaning "to undo, loosen." Images that undo, or loosen one's conscious perception of oneself are the basis by which the psyche heals itself.

April 15: * The Celtic month of the Willow Moon is April 15 to May 15. Lavendar is the sacred scent of this month, and it was thought that picking lavendar during full moon enhanced its powers.

The power of lavendar was known in several ancient civilizations. The ancient Greeks dedicated lavendar to Hecate, goddess of witches, sorcerers and enchantment, and later, the Romans burned it over hot coals to surround a new mother and child with the scent of compassion. Monks in medieval times wore sprigs of lavendar to banish evil spirits.

April 16: * From Plato's *Phaedrus* (279b), Socrates offers this prayer to Pan: "Beloved Pan, and all you other Gods who haunt this place, give me beauty in the inward soul; and may the outward and inward man be at one." Socrates, barefooted, is reclining on the shady banks of a river near a place sacred to nymphs. At the beginning, Socrates mentions that he is still struggling with the maxim, "know thyself" and with his sense of ignorance about his true nature. At the end comes his prayer with its appeal for inner beauty and by inference an end to ignorance, for in Platonic phychology, insight into the true nature of things brings true beauty. It is as if Pan (instincts) is the answer to the Apollonic question about self-knowledge. Psyche and instinct are inseparable. What we do to our instinct, we also do to our soul.

Socrates' prayer is still relevant. We can't find our way back to harmony with nature through study alone. In order to restore, conserve, and promote nature "out there," nature "in here" must also be restored, conserved, promoted. Otherwise, our perceptions of nature, our actions upon it, and our reactions to it, will continue to show the same mangled exaggerations of inadequate instinct.

* Music carries the body out of its separated loneliness. It educates (literally, "leads out") the soul driven into itself by fear. Dance styles began in the animal world; humans first learned motions and gestures from animals. Dance comes from the wild. Strict Biblical societies have been horrified by dance. A while back, it was polkas or waltzes, then foxtrots and charlestons, then jitterbug and the dirty imports: tango, rhumba, lambada. Dance had to be chaperoned, denounced, forbidden. The horror of dance is Hebrewism versus Hellenism; control versus spontaneity.

If our society suffers the disease of wild rapaciousness, it is because society has forgotten how to dance with nature.

This leads back to Socrates' puzzlings at the opening of the *Phaedrus* (230a). He considers his likeness to Typhon, a demonic giant of volcanic eruptions and earthquakes, "the personification of nature's destructive power." To "know thyself" in the *Phaedrus* begins with insight into nature's wild, unfettered aspect.

April 17: * The illusions in nightmares are so strongly impressed upon the mind that, even on waking, we may find it impossible not to believe they are real. The nightmare is a revelation of the fundamental nature of the human who as a sexual being is at one with animal being, instinct, and thus at one with nature. We too are pure nature. In nightmare the reality of the natural God is revealed.

April 18: * Folklore in the Dorset village of Tolpuddle says that the Topuddle Martyrs, agricultural laborers who were transported to Australia as criminals for forming a workers' association, were sheltered under a large sycamore tree while waiting to be shipped out in 1834. Because these martyrs are considered pioneers of the trade union movement, the tree was known as the Tolpuddle Martyrs' tree and is to this day a symbol of the labor movement. However, many have questioned whether the tree could possibly be that old. Now the National Trust of Britain, using a new method of dating trees without felling them, has established that the tree is actually 320 years old!

April 19: * The Old English word for a ball of thread is "clew." That's where we get the word clue. A clue is a thread that a seeker traces back to the center, looking for answers. In the Greek story of Theseus, the hero has won the love of Ariadne, daughter of the tyrant King Minos of Crete. Minos sets up a trap for Theseus: he must enter the Labyrinth and return. Ariadne goes for help to Daedalus, who designed the Labyrinth. He suggests the simplest solution: a ball of thread. She holds one end while Theseus winds through the Labyrinth. He is able to find his way back from certain death because of the thread that binds him to her.

April 20: * In myths, the hero's *ordeal* signifies the death of the ego. The hero is now aware that he is part of the cosmos. The old boundaries of the Self have been transcended. In some cases, the ego becomes a god with divine ability to rise above death and see the connectedness of all things. Greeks call this moment *apotheosis*, a step beyond *enthusiasm* (where you merely have the god in you). In a state of apotheosis, having tasted death, you *are* the god. After that, others may see the hero differently, too. This is sometimes called a moment of *epiphany*. The Catholic Feast of the Epiphany on January 6 celebrates the moment when the Magi first realized the divinity of the newborn Christ.

The chain of divine experience is from *enthusias*m, being visited by a god, to *apotheosis*, becoming a god, to *epiphany*, being recognized as a god. Heroes themselves may experience epiphany; a hero may realize suddenly, after a supreme ordeal, that he is the son of a god, a chosen one with special powers.

James Joyce expanded the meaning, to a sudden perception of the essence, seeing to the core of a person, idea, or thing.

April 21: * On Crete during the Bronze Age, from about 2500 B.C. to after 1500 B.C., the culture of the Minoans flourished. In comparison to the religion of the Greeks, certain characteristic traits of Minoan religion emerge in surviving artifacts. One is the preponderance of goddesses and of female cult officiants. Masculine deities are scarce in comparison, and masculine cult images are lacking altogether. The most recognizable cults are that of the household serpent goddesses and the nature cult in both of its two aspects: the Lady and Lord of Beasts and that of Trees. All phallic symbols, such as abound and are so aggressive in numerous other religions, including the historic religion of Greece, are completely absent in Minoan art. The culture was apparently matriarchal. The grace and elegance of the ladies in Minoan art represent a civilized refinement that has not been equaled since. Before the arrival of the Greeks in Crete, there were no walled cities. No battle scenes are depicted. The tone is of general luxury and delight, a broad participation by all classes in a genial atmosphere of well-being, and the vast development of a profitable commerce by sea.

* The image of mother and female affects the psyche differently from that of father and male. Where the mother image predominates, even the dualism of life and death dissolves in the rapture of her solace; the worlds of nature and spirit are not separated; the plastic arts flourish without need of explanation, allegory or moral; and there is a tacit confidence in the spontaneity of nature, both in its killing, sacrificial aspect, and in its reproductive, productive aspect.

April 22: * I have read that a miracle is not the suspension of natural law, but the operation of a higher law.

* Modern depth psychology emerged out of 19th century disciplines (psychiatry, anthropology, folklore, spiritualism, comparative religion, and mythology), all or some of which influenced the unconscious. The comparative study of motifs is a basic tenet of depth psychology and a basic method employed by all psychoanalytic investigations from Roheim through Neumann. Depth psychology turns to mythology to understand ourselves in the present. We can't touch myth without its touching us. The massive research of the 19th century greats led to the recognition that humanity was not only Western, modern, secular, civilized, and sane, but also primitive, archaic, mythical, magical, and mad. A new relativism had to be faced: there were other myths influencing behavior than the Bible, other Gods than Christ, other people than white, and within

each individual, there were other kinds of consciousness with diverse intentions and values.

James Hollis: "For more than 2000 years, Judeo-Christianity has bent its will toward the repression of our pagan past which, thanks to Roscher, was not lost but is preserved in the *Lexikon.*" The polytheistic imagination he catalogues plays a role in our behavior equal with reason and feeling because it is still in our genes. Hollis says, "When Christ was the operative myth, it was enough to know his modes and those of the Devil. Now that this single model of consciousness has dissociated into the root multiples which lay dormant below it and which are present in mythology, we need to include mythological reflection upon our attitudes and behavior."

April 23: * Thomas Rymous of Erceldoune (C. 1220-c.1297), known as Thomas the Rymer, became widely known after his book of prophecies was published in 1603. One of his rhymes was:

When Tweed and Powsail meet at Merlin's grave,
Scotland and England shall one monarch have.

April 24: * Chloe Ardelia Wofford was the second of four children of George and Ramah Wofford of Lorain, Ohio. During her childhood, the family lived in at least six apartments, one of which was set on fire by the landlord when the family couldn't pay their rent of four dollars a month. When Chloe was twelve years old, she converted to Catholicism, taking the name of Anthony as her baptismal name, after St. Anthony. She later shortened it to Toni and married Harold Morrison, a Jamaica-born architect. 1993, Toni Morrison became the first African-American to win the Nobel Prize for Literature.

April 25: * Diamonds are three billion years old. They are the oldest substance known to man.

* Ron Reagan, about his father's funeral: "Cheney brought my mother up to the casket...she has glaucoma and has trouble seeing. There were steps, and he left her there. He just stood there, letting her flounder. I don't think he's a mindful human being."

April 26: * The Intuit Eskimo artisan meditates on each stone or tusk he intends to carve until its reality begins to emerge in his mind. He takes his time in considering a piece of stone, spending a long time, sometimes several months, studying it, allowing his thoughts to crystallize before he picks up his tools.

April 27: * The first time I took Bill to visit my family in Amarillo, it was the mid-1980s. We were eating in a coffee shop. Bill observed the men a while and said, "I've never seen so many giants in my life!" Sure enough, there were a lot of very big men. We jokingly attributed it to the fact that we were in beef country. As it turns out, we may not have been too far wrong. Height, it has been proven, is more closely aligned to early nutrition than it is to genetics.

Over the past 30 years that data has been gathered, they have concluded that height is a kind of biological shorthand: a composite code for all factors that make up a society's well-being. Height variations within a population are largely genetic, but variations between populations are mostly environmental. So the U.N. uses height to monitor nutrition in developing countries.

The dean of anthroprometric historians is U. of Munich Prof. John Komlos. For 20 years he has gathered data on both sides of the Atlantic from hundreds of sources. For centuries, governments have kept careful records of soldiers' heights, and these are among his data. His team found that in Northern Europe over the past 1200 years, human growth has followed a U-shaped curve: from a high around 800 A.D. to a low in the 17th century, and back up again. Charlemagne, for example, was well over six feet; whereas, the soldiers who stormed the Bastille 1000 years later averaged a mere five feet tall and weighed 100 pounds.

Biologists say we achieve our stature in three spurts: the first in infancy, the second between the ages of six and eight, the last in adolescence. Oldest grandson Daniel just reached that age, and when I saw him last, he had shot up to six feet three inches! I'm often amazed by the amount of food he can put away.

From the end of World War II to the end of the century, economists have called America the richest country in the world. But by other indices—longevity, income inequality, and crime—it now trails Northern Europe and Japan.

As for women, the National Center for Health Statistics shows, in a study of 35,000 women, those born in the late 1950s and early 1960s average just under five-feet-five. Those born a decade later are a third of an inch shorter.

A mentor of Komlos's, U of Chicago Economics Nobelist Robert Fogel, questioned prevailing wisdom that people grow taller and faster the wealthier their country. He found that, because Southern plantation owners wanted to get the most work done, their slaves were fed and housed nearly as well as white Northern farmers. One of Fogel's graduate students, Richard Steckel, went through more than 10,000 slave manifests to find heights of 50,000 slaves. He found that adult slaves were nearly as tall as free whites and three to five inches taller than the average Africans back in Africa.

Steckel also found that men of the northern Cheyenne tribe were the tallest people in the world in the late 19th century. They ate well on bison and berries, and wandered clear of disease on the high plains. He enlisted anthropologists to gather bone measurements dating back 10,000 years. In both Europe and the Americas, humans grew shorter as their cities grew larger.

Komlos tabulated heights of 140,000 Austrian soldiers and their children, 10,742 American slaves, servants, soldiers and apprentices in the early 1700s, 4180 West Point graduates, and 38,000 French soldiers from the late 1700s onward. Of the latter, he found that peasant conscripts were nearly three inches shorter than their well-fed officers. Which could explain the French Revolution.

America was a good place to live in the 18th century. Game was abundant, land was free for the clearing, settlement was sparse enough to prevent epidemics. Then around the mid-1800s, heights shrank. But by the end of the 19th century, heights edged up again.

Then something strange happened. While heights in Europe continued to climb, the U.S. remained unchanged. In World War I, the average G.I. was still two inches taller than the average German. But around 1955, Germans and other Europeans began to grow an extra two centimeters a decade, and some Asian populations grew several times more, so that now, the Japanese—once the shortest industrialized people on earth—have nearly caught up with us, and Northern Europeans are three inches taller than we are and are still climbing. Life expectancy charts comparing 37 industrialized nations show that Americans rank 28th in longevity, the Japanese being first.

The obvious answer would seem to be immigration. But Komlos only included native-born Americans who speak English in the home, and he did not include people of Asian and Hispanic descent in his study. In any case, Steckel says, the U.S. takes in too few immigrants to account for the disparity with Northern Europe. In the 19th century, when we were the world's tallest people, we took in floods of malnourished immigrants. But after three generations, the immigrants catch up. Around the world, well-fed children differ in height by less than half an inch.

Animals in cold climates tend to have larger bodies and shorter limbs than those in warm climates. But although climate still shapes animals, its effect on industrialized people has almost disappeared. Swedes ought to be short and stocky, yet now they are some of the world's tallest people. Mexicans ought to be tall and slender, yet they're often stunted by poor diet. By 2000, Maya who moved to the U.S. were four inches taller than Guatemalan Maya. They weren't genetically small; they were malnourished. Protestants are taller than Catholics because the families have fewer mouths to feed.

April 28: * Each hell we go through burns off more illusions. In the back of *Forbes* magazine I once read a quote from Lucie Delarue Mardus (but have never been able to discover who she is, or was): "Life consists of subtractions: things you have to give up."

* Holland's growth spurt began only in the mid-1800s, when its first liberal democracy was established. Before 1850, the country grew rich off its colonies, but the wealth stayed in the hands of the wealthy, and the average citizen's shrank. In a true democracy, when the G.NP grows, everyone grows. Inequality may be at the root of America's current height stagnation. Americans lose the most height to Northern Europeans in infancy and adolescence, which implicates pre- and post-natal care and teenage eating habits.

April 29: * Ed Laufer, my late father-in-law, was a Wall Street brokerage analyst who lost money, so they say, only on the day he died. The reason? He died before he could sell; he died sitting at his desk. Every day he commuted by train to work in Manhattan from his home in South Orange. He was 83 years old. Quite a man.

* Wall Street got its name in this way: during colonial times,

farmers built a long wall in what is now Lower Manhattan to prevent free-roaming hogs from trampling their fields. This former pig pen is now called Wall Street.

April 30: * According to James Hollis, "The history of relation between the sexes is a sad litany of men seeking to dominate and control because of their fear of the feminine within themselves."

Sometimes a man controlled by fear will try to keep "her" (wife, mother, female figure) happy, sacrificing his own well-being in the process. Or he tries to get his way but avoids confrontation by passive-aggressive behavior that seeks control and revenge.

* Thomas Jefferson's Ten Rules:

1) Never put off until tomorrow what you can do today.
2) Never trouble another for what you can do yourself.
3) Never spend money before you have earned it.
4) Never buy what you don't want because it is cheap.
5) Pride costs more than hunger, thirst and cold.
6) We seldom repent of having eaten too little.
7) Nothing is troublesome that we do willingly.
8) How much pain the evils cost us that never happened.
9) Take things always by the smooth handle.
10) If angry, count 10 before speaking; if very angry, count 100.

* Who wrote *Enthusiasm Makes the Difference*? Must be Norman Vincent Peale. I'm remembering how "enthusiastic" describes son Jeff. When he was at Rice, he was hospitalized for a retina repair. (Never mind about the water balloon war that led to the discovery of holes in the retina.) Lamar, Tucker and I went to see him in the hospital, and he had his cytology book open, trying to infect us with his enthusiasm for the magical mystery of cells while our eyes glazed over. *Of course* he became a doctor!

Before Hurricane Rita, to get his family to safety, Jeff drove Linda, their twins Gregory and Elizabeth, the two dogs, their *snake*, and their *hermit crab* to Austin—a 23-hour trip due to traffic jams. The snake escaped, roaming the car until finally climbing onto Linda's shoulder. Is that an enthusiastic bunch, or what? Nothing gets them down.

May:

May 1: * The Celtic holiday of Beltane, celebrated on May 1, is when Celt extinguished hearth fires in their homes and kindled their bel-fires (made of nine sacred woods) on hilltops. Then they formed rings and danced clockwise around them. They relit their hearthfires with burning brands (samhnags) from the hilltop fires. Then they drove their cattle into the hilltop embers. (One of the sacred woods was calton, or hazel, which gave its name to an ancient law hill, Calton Hill in Edinburgh. Rowans and mountain ash were planted near doorways to keep out evil spirits. Aspen and thorn were never used for building, because these trees were inhabited by fairies.) Over their newly-lit hearth fires they boiled cauldrons of fresh spring water, which they sprinkled over the floors of every building in use.

In the Highlands, near Kingussie, a hardboiled egg or bannock, marked with a cross (life) on one side and a circle (death) on the other, was rolled down a hill down three times, and when it came to rest, the owner had to determine what sign turned up most often.

Divination is easier. We have a destiny of our own making to fulfill. Our destiny is a promise we made to ourselves when we were around nine or ten. I may forget that promise, but my inner child never forgets, and I will never be at peace until I honor the promise. If I don't keep it, I betray myself, the person I could be. Then I had better keep a close rein on myself, put myself in narrow confines, because there will be chaos inside. To discover what love would have me do with my life, I note my natural abilities. When I remember the promise and begin to honor it, *magic* begins to happen.

The first breakthrough to realization of a meaning in one's life—the discovery of the work one loves to do—may come early, often in childhood. The recognition of a skill, or an ability to "create" in one sphere or another, allows us to set free our *daeman* (or Ariel, as he is called in Shakespeare's *The Tempest*). The outer forms of this "calling" may change often, even dramatically, along the way, but the root remains the same. Ariel will create or destroy in obedience to these goals. The task of the middle years is to uncover the differing motives behind our various activities and realize how they are conditioned by the hidden fantasy life in the unconscious.

May 2: * On May 2, in many parts of Scotland, honeysuckle is, or was, placed in cowsheds to prevent the cattle inside from being influenced by the curses of witches.

* Anthropometric historians have studied hundreds of thousands of height records from the past twelve hundred years—never possible before computers, no matter how many graduate assistants there were. They discovered The Netherlands has become a land of giants. In a century's time, the Dutch have gone from being among the smallest people in Europe to the largest in the world. Another series of studies has shown that tall men earn more money over a lifetime, are more likely to be elected to public office, and marry earlier.

May 3: * There is a statement in the Old Testament where Wisdom plays around the throne of God, as a child plays with total concentration. I remember once when his brothers were gone, Tucker got up into the climbing tower out of sight of his parents, who were sitting by the pool. We could hear him at his solitary play, which we guessed to be a great battle of the warrior against evil forces. This went on for a very long time, until I began to wonder if he was having some kind of fit. But he was just totally lost in his play.

Collectively, we've lost the wonder of stones and soil, of animals and birds, and we've lost the spontaneous voices of dream and vision, without which the people perish. We long to return to the gifts of our mother the earth.

May 4: * If you're far enough away from something, you can relate to it at a much more intimate level than to something that is just pulsing with intimacy. There's a paradox there. We sense ourselves poised on a pinhead between the transitory and the eternal worlds. T. S. Eliot says, "Except for the point, the still point,/ There would be no dance, and there is only the dance." At the jumping-off place on the point of the paradox, all truth lives. Again from Eliot, it's "A condition of complete simplicity/ (Costing not less than everything)."

May 5: * In Celtic myth, Ceridwen and her husband, the king, have a son who is so ugly that they name him Afaggdu (Welsh for "utter darkness"). She knows he'll never be accepted as he is in the court of the High King, so she decides to make him so wise that everyone will seek him. Following directions from a magic book, she gathers rare herbs at certain times of the moon and boils them in a cauldron over the period of a year and a day, to concoct a magic potion that must cook down to three drops containing the essence of wisdom. Since she can't constantly keep the fire going and stir the pot by herself, she hires an old blind man who happens along, led by a young bumbling guide. He stirs the pot while the boy, Gwion Bach, feeds the fire with wood collected nearby. This leaves Ceridwen to gather the herbs at the specified times as laid out in the spell book.

Finally the potion is ready. Ceridwen has stationed her ugly son next to the cauldron to drink the potion, while she sits down to wait beneath a tree. But at the crucial moment, she falls asleep, and instead of her son Afaggdu, it is the boy Gwion Bach who gets the three drops. When she wakes, she is furious. But Gwion, who now possesses all the world's wisdom, realizes she will destroy him in her rage, and runs away. Ceridwen gives chase. Gwion changes shape, becoming various animals, but each time, Ceridwen also changes into the appropriate predator. Finally he changes into a kernel of corn, but she becomes a hen and eats the corn.

With the corn seed in her belly, she becomes pregnant. Now she waits until the baby is born, so that she can kill him. But when the baby comes, he is so beautiful that she can't. Neither can she keep him because he has robbed Afaggdu of his chance of acceptance. She takes Gwion to the sea and sets him adrift in a tiny coracle. Eventually a prince rescues him and names him Taliesin, "the radiant bow," because he shines with beauty and wisdom.

No more is said of poor Afaggdu in this story, but he reappears as King Arthur's right-hand man in a battle. In that story, he needs no armor because coarse, stiff hair protects his body.

May 6: * *Humor,* in the Middle Ages and through the Renaissance, meant, among other things, one of the four principal body fluids that determine human dispositions and health (sanguine, phlegmatic, choleric, melancholic). In physiology it still means "any clear or hyaline (transparent) body fluid such as blood, lymph, or bile." The root is the Latin *umor* meaning "liquid, fluid." So humor is something that flows, and humors are unconscious drives. But a *sense* of humor means more. *Sense* means "a capacity to appreciate or understand."

There's a difference between mere reaction to something comical and a sense of humor, which connotes a sense of proportion. There are many kinds of laughter, and some of it conceals contempt or a desire to hurt. The word *humility* must have a relationship to *humor*, because one with a sense of humor is unassuming and sees the underlying humor in one's *own* situation, not in the misfortune of someone else. In other words, we can see laughter at the heart of things. Schiller says, "Man is only fully human when he is at play."

May 7: * Haggis is banned in the USA. The FDA says it is unfit for human consumption, but in Scotland, queues form for "offal and oatmeal trapped in sheep's stomachs." In fact, there's a recipe for the perfect Scotch breakfast: a bottle of whisky, a haggis, and a collie dog. The collie dog is for eating the haggis.

*Friend/philosopher/playwright Olivia Orfield: "The demonic is never more terrible than when it appears in rational guise."

May 8: * External reality is absolutely indifferent to our fate. The world does not give itself spontaneously. It must be taken.

* Jung said that one should not see in the extroverted modality the only possibility of rapport with the world. In other words, whether it takes place by an inner or outer search, what matters is to reach a precise awareness of our own objectives. When this happens, all the obstacles we meet will be seen as components of the same searching and not as malevolence on the part of the world. Neuroticism is linked to a vision of the world as an indestructible, everlasting enemy.

May 9: * A fundamental condition of life is that it does not allow itself to be reduced to anything precise, so the question about the meaning of life must remain unanswered. Hence the importance of the *riddle,* the *paradox,* as a life archetype. In truth, the hero isn't the brave, well-put-together type. The one who is sent to fight the monsters is a person already suffering, discontented, depressed. He grasps at some level all the contradictions in his life. He may be the child who behind the superficially correct behavior of his parents is able to sense their unexpressed conflicts. He will become the so-called neurotic: the bearer of the family's hardships: the scapegoat.

The power to mold reality in such a way that it functions

satisfactorily lies in the hands of each person. This possibility of shaping one's life saves one from neurosis; otherwise, the sufferer remains in a passive situation in the face of everything that happens. It is our passivity that gives the world that malign appearance that frightens us so much. Our neuroses are the real powers. W. H. Auden said: "We are lived by Powers we pretend to understand."

May 10: * After having faced dangers of every kind and slain the "dragon," the "hero" comes into possession of the "treasure". Here a new problem arises that concerns the use of this treasure. We can trace three basic models. One type of hero is the extrovert, who seeks to expand his role in the world and use his strength and intelligence to transform reality. He confronts the dragon on the outside, in the reality that surrounds him, and that is where he fights his battles. The introverted hero seeks to introduce inward values: Socrates, Buddha or Jesus offered new visions of the world. Introverted heroes discover within themselves a truth, a value, and try to communicate it to the world. The introvert deals in the world of ideas. The third type of hero doesn't seek to change the world through struggles either on the outside on inside, but to transform the personality. The growth of individuality is the answer to the perils of the soul that threaten from within and to perils of the world that threaten from without. To know and transform themselves is the task of those who experience the dialogue between nature and culture. Psychic reality is where inner and outer come together.

May 11: * Another tragedy of our invasion of Iraq: During her lirfetime, Gertrude Bell, the Englishwoman celebrated in *Desert Queen,* was instrumental in establishing the Iraq Museum to preserve the history of ancient Mesopotamia between the Tigris and Euphrates rivers, the cradle of Western civilization—from designing the building to acquiring its collections. When she died in 1926, in her will she bequeathed fifty thousand pounds—an enormous sum at that time—to enlarge the collection. Archeologists spent their entire lives collecting and cataloguing artifacts for posterity. In April 2003, the museum was sacked by looters and its collections stolen or destroyed.

May 12: * A total of 63 thanedoms once existed in Scotland. Saxons adopted the Norse word *thegn*, meaning a trusted servant of the king. The most notable thane today is the young Thane of Cawdor, whose lair above a rocky burn is Cawdor Castle, between Nairn and Culloden's bloody battlefield. The Charter of Thanage was first received by Robert the Bruce in 1310 by one William Calder. The Calders are said to be descended from a brother of Macbeth, who was king from 1040 to1057. The building of the Tower of Calder, which is the heart of the present Cawdor Castle, began in 1454.

The ninth thane was actually a woman, a thaness named Muriel. In 1499, when Muriel was a small child, she was out walking near the tower with her nurse when she was captured by a party of 60 Campbells. When the nurse realized what they were about to do, fearing the child would lose her identity and her right to the thanedom, she bit off a joint of Muriel's little finger and scarred her hip with a key, all to mark her as the rightful heiress. Her uncles rode out to rescue her, but Campbell of Innerliever, who saw them coming, turned over a kettle and put his own seven sons to defend the kettle until death. Then he took off with the child and the nurse. The Calders slew all seven sons, but when they turned over the kettle, no Muriel was found. By that time, Campbell was too far away to pursue. The nurse's precaution of marking the true heiress was well-founded. Campbell of Auchinbreck, when asked what they would do if the girl died before she came of marriageable age, said, "She can never die as long as a red-haired lassie can be found on either side of Loch Awe." But she didn't die, so no imposter took her place. In 1510 she married Sir John Campbell, third son of the second Earl of Argyll, and from this union descended the Campbells of Calder, created Baron Cawdor in 1796 and Earl Cawdor of Castlemartin in 1827.

Aside: Shakespeare's Macbeth wasn't actually the Thane of Cawdor, but a Thane of Glamis. The late sixth Earl of Cawdor said of this blunder: "As Cawdor Castle was not built until the late fourteenth century, it is impossible for King Duncan to have lost any blood or Lady Macbeth much less sleep in this particular house."

May 13: * Contrary to what evangelicals insist, biologists tell us homosexuality is a biologically based orientation that has existed in roughly the same percentages throughout history. The Kinsey Report of the 1960s or 70s showed that it also exists in cattle, for example.

In recent years researchers have even found the "gay" gene. The genetic spin of the dice is engineered by that same god worshipped by the fundamentalists who supplant love with fear and oppression. Jungian analyst James Hollis says it's time to come out of the macho closet and name the real problem: men fear those who incarnate their unlived life. The enemy is not the other guy. As Pogo said, "We have met the enemy and he is us." One of my favorite poets, Pablo Neruda, wrote, "It so happens I am sick of being a man."

May 14: * One of my great-grandparents was named McNabb, which is why I found this interesting: In Scotland, "Doing a MacNab" (different spellings but the same name) means achieving a feat by a character in John Buchan's 1925 novel, *John MacNab*. You have to catch a salmon and shoot a brace of grouse by lunchtime and bag a stag before dinner. If you get a woman as well during the day, you have achieved a Royal McNab. This has nothing to do with my McNabb ancestors, who have been gone from Scotland and Ireland for several centuries—except the grouse part. I was told by my aunt that Great-Grandpa McNabb groused about everything!

May 15: * The saint day for Isidore, patron saint of farmers (c. 1070-1130) whose fields were plowed by angels while he prayed.

* "Calm" is a Gaelic word which literally means "sanctuary." It is an imaginary circle drawn around a body with the hand which serves as a ring of protection.

* "Spinster" came into the printed language in 1362. It was the occupation of a spinner of wool into yarn on a spinning wheel. Men in occupations like brewing or weaving were called "brewsters" or "websters" and they took these as proper names. But the spinster's work was not socially elevating. By the 17th century, English law made it the legal designation of an unmarried woman, which had less stigma than "old maid" or "maiden lady," meaning virginity.

May 16: * The Vikings weren't the first inhabitants of the Shetlands. The archaeological site at Jarlshof, on Mainland, derives its name from that of the laird's house in Sir Walter Scott's *The Pirate*. Over 3,500 years ago this was the location of a settlement (between 200 and 100 B.C.) which was later taken over by the Vikings.

May 17: * According to Jordanis and Cassidor, the race of Huns originated from an intermixture of fauni ficarii (either incubi or satyres or silvestres—wood spirits) with witch-like women. Ficarii has been linked to fig. In both Sicilian folk songs and Greek superstition, even today fig trees are reputed to be the seats of evil spirits. Perhaps the indecent meaning of fig (Italian fica, French figue) is in context here.

May 18: * From a history written in 1521 by John Major, or Mair, (1469-1550), we learn that during the reign of the emperor Claudius, a war broke between the Scots and Picts on one side and the Romans and Britons on the other. The war, lasting 154 years, was aimed at bringing Scots and Picts into subjugation. The Romans and Britons spared no woman or child as they leveled several cities, including Agned. The city was rebuilt by Heth, king of the Picts, and came to be known as Hethburg, which gradually became Edinburgh.

May 19: * The Latin word for "painted" is *pictus*, which is where the name "Picts" came from. These fine, wild, fierce people only inherited through the female line (the matrilinear system) and intermarried in groups of four lineages—a practice found in ancient creation myths. There are about 320 "Pit" place-names in Scotland, which are all that remain of the Picts. Nobody knows where they came from (they were first mentioned by Roman orator and teacher Eumenius in 297) or why they vanished so suddenly after 843, when they were united with the Scots under Kenneth mac Alpin.

May 20: * Figure this one out: In Lebanon, men are legally allowed to have sex with animals, but the animals must be female. Having sexual relations with a male animal is punishable by death.

* In Bahrain, a male doctor may legally examine a woman's genitals, but is prohibited from looking directly at them. He may only see their reflection in a mirror.

* Muslims are banned from looking at the genitals of a corpse. This also applies to undertakers; the sex organs of the deceased must be covered with a brick or piece of wood at all times.

* In Hong Kong, a betrayed wife is legally allowed to kill her adulterous husband, but only with her bare hands. The husband's

lover, on the other hand, may be killed in any manner desired.

* Topless saleswomen are legal in Liverpool, England, but only in tropical fish stores.

* In Cali, Colombia, a woman may only have sex with her huband, and the first time, her mother must be in the room as witness.

* In Maryland, it is illegal to sell condoms from vending machines with one exception: only "in places where alcoholic beverages are sold for consumption on the premises."

May 21: * Jung disagreed with Freud about sex being the strongest drive in humankind. Jung believed that hunger is the strongest drive. "Sex comes only after hunger is satisfied," he said.

* On May 21, 1927, Charles A. Lindbergh landed his "Spirit of St. Louis" near Paris, completing the first solo airplane flight across the Atlantic Ocean.

May 22: * For hundreds of years Christian historians who wrote our textbooks portrayed Genghis Khan as a savage. In the early 13th century, he and his Mongol army subjugated more lands and people than the Romans did in 40 years. However, modern historians show that he was a charismatic leader with a brilliant understanding of both warfare and human nature. The Mongol invasion connected much of Asian civilization and bridged Asia and Europe, preparing the way for the Renaissance.

May 23: * A miracle is a momentous event that seems to come from nowhere against all odds. We never have to look far for a miracle, from the bumblebee with its too-heavy body that flies nonetheless, to our mind and body, which carry out numerous complex functions every second. Life itself is a miracle that nobody has yet explained. As a child I used to wonder about so many things that I believed I would understand fully when I grew up. (I remember the old song, "You'll understand it all by and by.") It turns out that there are many things I'll never understand. Somehow I find that comforting.

May 24: * There is a phenomenon where people who work together for a while actually start to function as a whole, a sort of collective state of flow. It's part of the phenomenon of entrainment, where for example, women who live together begin to experience their menstrual cycle at the same time of the month. And there is a phenomenon of thought, wherein, as physicist David Bohm wrote, "Thought creates the world and then says, 'I didn't do it.'" Bohm described a "generative order" in which we "participate in how reality unfolds." But sometimes patterns of thought hold us captive. We tend to see ourselves as separate from our environment. We need to be open to fundamental shifts of mind: from seeing a world made up of things (separating ourselves from life) to seeing a world made up of relationships. When we think of ourselves as part of the unfolding of things, we begin to experience "synchronicity." We begin to think of relationship as the organizing principle of the universe, according to Leon Jaworski's son Joseph, who, with Betty Sue Flowers, has written a book about the phenomenon.

May 25: * On May 25, 1925, John T. Scopes was indicted in Tennessee for teaching Darwin's theory of evolution. This confirmed for much of the U.S. ouside the Deep South what a backward place Appalachia was. The term "hillbilly" became a popular description.

May 26: * Psychologists say when a relationship is born of an attraction that we're unable to account for in any way, as soon as passion is gone, all that remains is a sense of emptiness and futility, as though there's nothing to say to each other. To stay in this situation, even trying to justify it by an undefined feeling about custom, means a kind of inner death for both. If there is a divorce at this point, the woman often wants to give some gift to the man. It might be money, or the house, or the dog. It's as if she were trying to assuage her guilt for abandoning him.

May 27: * Someone named Jim Maclachlan said: "Dialogue is the oxygen of change."

* A ray of sunlight is symbolic of the awareness that sets us apart from others. It also symbolizes the arrow that wounds us.

* What is the difference, if any, between life and consciousness? Psychiatrist Gordon R. Globus says: "...all matter which embodies events is conscious—or perhaps better, protoconscious—as a function of the complexity and parameters of the event embodied by

the particular matter. Although it may seem absurd to propose that all organizations are conscious, this apparent absurdity may reflect human chauvinism about consciousness." ("Unexpected Symmetries in the World Knot," *Science,* 1980.)

Kenneth R. Pelletier, commenting on the same subject: "This proposal is not a naive, pantheistic attribution of a human type consciousness to inanimate matter or other animal organisms. Each level of organization in matter represents an aspect of potential consciousness directly propotional to its porision in the evolutionary chain—from inorganic matter to sentience." (*Toward a Science of Consciousness*. NY: Dell, 1978.)

May 28: * When I was a child, I used to hug trees, a fact Lamar couldn't imagine. I listened to their heart. When I was older, I learned there are lots of tree huggers in the world. Which leads to this:

* Recently a U.S. reporter challenged Russian president Vladimir Putin, saying his country's elections weren't democratic. Putin shot back that the U.S. has one of the most undemocratic systems of voting in the so-called free world. This criticism has been made by some of our stauchest allies: our electoral college system simply isn't democratic. At our country's onset, founders believed that backwoods citizens could not possibly make an informed decision about the most qualified candidate and this should be decided by an electoral college of learned men. Maybe there was logic in this rationale then, but now we have widespread access to information about candidates, and although there are many uneducated people, if we truly believe that all are created equal, then it's about time to revamp our system and let every person's vote count equally.

One man won 50,999,897 votes for the Presidency, more than any Democrat in history, more than any candidate in history except Reagan in 1984, and *more than half a million more votes than the man who assumed office*. We can only speculate what would have happened if the Supreme Court had refused to determine the election, or if conservatives on Supreme Court had not outnumbered liberals by a single vote. Without getting into personalities of the candidates, because we are not a true democracy, the majority of the American people were deprived their choice.

Then certain radical religious groups claimed a "mandate" from

God. One would think, if God were in charge of the election, He could devise a fairer system.

Which gets back to me: where does a fiscally conservative tree-hugger, who opposes preemptive war, who believes in a balanced budget, separation of church and state, and equal rights for all, go?

May 29: * On a daily, intimate level, Pueblo Indians see their rituals as instrumental in helping the sun to rise. When people feel they're living a symbolic life, that they're actors in a divine drama, they're at peace. Their lives are meaningful. Without meaningful rites, we suffer from deep wounds to the soul: life without depth.

* Auburn U. History Prof. Wayne Flint wrote a book, *Dixie's Forgotten People* (Indiana U. Press, 1979, 2004), about the South's poor whites who slid deep into poverty after the Civil War and have never escaped. Flint says Southern poor whites are the one American minority that it is safe to hold up to public ridicule. Protestant residents of the Bible Belt, mostly Anglo-Saxon in origin, they form part of the most ethnically homogeneous region in the U.S. They have been isolated from mainstream white Southern culture and have in turn been stereotyped by the dominant culture as rednecks and Holy Rollers (referring to Pentecostal and holiness religion they embrace). They have been discriminated against and misunderstood. In their isolation, they have developed a unique subculture and have defended it with a tenacity and pride that puzzles and confuses others. This is a fascinating study that Americans should read. We know African, Hispanic or Amerindian cultures much better than this one.

May 30: * M. Scott Peck says marriage is like a mountain climbers' base camp, a place where there is shelter and provisions, where climbers can rest before setting out for the next part of the climb. "Successful climbers know they must spend at least as much time, if not more, in tending to their base camp as they actually do in climbing mountains...." In marriage, both must tend to each other before they venture forth; both tend the hearth, both venture forth.

* Jeff Gannon masqueraded as a reporter at White House news briefings for two years before it was discovered that his news organization was a front for GOP activists and that his most impressive portfolio had been as a model in ads for an escort service.

But there's a bigger issue here than Mr. Gannon. The Washington press corps' eagerness to facilitate and serve as dress extras in what amounted to an administration promotional video can now be seen as a metaphor for how much the legitimate press was co-opted by all manner of fakery. How dangerous is that?

"Our once noble calling," wrote Philip Meyer in *The Columbia Journalism Review*, "is increasingly difficult to distinguish from things that look like journalism but are primarily advertising, press agentry or entertainment." You know we're in trouble when Jeff Gannon, asked about his murky past on Bill Maher's show on April 29, moralistically joked that "usually the way it works is people become reporters before they prostitute themselves."

May 31: * Yearly, *Parade* Magazine does a survey called "What America Earns." In 2003 they reported that the gap between America's highest- and lowest-paid workers got wider. CEOs' average cash bonus alone was $605,000 in 2003, a 26% jump over 2002. CEOs now average more than $10 million a year in total compensation—370 times more than the average hourly worker gets.

* Mexican proverbs:

No hagas cosas buenas que parezcan malas.
(Don't do good that could look bad.)
Para tonto no se estudia.
(One needn't study to become a fool.)
Al nopal lo van a ver sólo cuando tiene tunas.
(The prickly pear has company only when it bears fruit.)
+ *El que come y canta, loco se levanta.*
(He who eats and sings, wakes up crazy.)
+ *El que cuida sus cosas, sus cosas lo cuidaron.*
(He who takes care of his things, his things take care of him.)
+ *Dime con quien andos y dirê quien eres.*
(Tell me with whom you walk and I'll tell you who you are.)
+ *El hombre con los manos en la bolsa no sirve para nada.*
(The man with his hands on his purse is good for nothing.)

+ The last four, given to me by Ida Luttrell, are from the *Jim Hogg County Enterprise.*

June

June 1: * In a far simpler time, the Dionne Quintuplets were born this week in 1934, first quints known to have survived infancy: Annette, Marie, Cecile, Emilie, and Yvonne. Canada made them wards of the state and placed them in a nursery tourist attraction called Quintland. Frequently, for many years, they made appearances on movie newsreels. We saw the quints often, not realizing these appearances were manditory. Only two quints are still living. Three sued the Ontario government for exploiting them, and in 1998 they were awarded four million dollars in damages.

June 2: * John Donne: "Nor ever chaste except You (God) ravish me (the poet)." In Jungian terms, an artist has to be ravished by the archetypal unconscious or there is no art. It's the artist's feminine side that is ravished by archetypal energy. But we must be careful not to allow the ego to be completely overcome. There's an insidious pull luring the ego into unconsciousness. It says, "Consciousness is too painful. Why not get fatter, sleepier, or drunker?" Listening to that voice will make us think we're too ugly, too worthless to live—and we must do something to justify our existence.

June 3: * One of the world's best timekeepers is the cicada. There are twelve broods of 17-year cicadas. The largest is Brood X, which last surfaced in 2004. A smaller one, Brood II, came out in 1996. There are also three broods of 13-year cicadas. Since cicadas spend most of their lives a foot underground, feeding on sap from tree roots, did they originate on this continent, or did they originate in Asia or Europe? If they didn't originate here, how did they get here?

June 4: * Claremont de Castillejo wrote that libido, or life energy, changes direction when old age approaches. Outer activities lose their appeal and the inner world demands attention. If their garden is as it should be, they can die content, feeling they have fulfilled their task of becoming the person they were born to be.

June 5: * Activity theory posits that people don't change their attitudes and lifestyles as they age. The implication of this is that most aging persons would choose to remain active if given the chance.

* Something I have learned: If we do not allow ourselves to feel our feelings, we will act them out. But if you ask a dozen people, "What are you feeling right now?" very few would be able to answer.

June 6: * Most people are driven to exhaustion by the ever-increasing demands made upon them for action, so that their first obligation, their most important responsibility, to set up the ladder between man and the Divine, between conscious and unconscious, takes last place in their list of priorities. Contemplation is not a separation from action, as every true contemplative and mystic has known; it is rather an attitude to both action and stillness, by which at last they are one. (Recall T. S. Eliot, from *The Four Quartets*: "At the still point, there the dance is.")

June 7: * On June 7, 1929, the sovereign state of Vatican City came into being as copies of the Lateran Treaty were exchanged in Rome.

* Alex Haley: "When an old person dies, it's like a library burning."

June 8: * The miracle that a female is able to produce a male out of herself was originally ascribed by primitive woman to the *numinosum*, to the wind, or the ancestral spirits.

* Mark Twain: "The radical of one century is the conservative of the next. The radical invents the views. When he has worn them out, the conservative adopts them."

June 9: * It is precisely the least important things that we must pay attention to. The *I Ching*, hexagram 57, says there is "success in small matters." Heraclites said, "The waking have one common world, but the sleeping turn aside each into a world of his own."

* Matthew Klam, quoting a friend: "The bloody thing about fiction is that it has to be true, but you have to make it up."

June 10: * In the Egyptian myth of Osiris, the god is killed and chopped to pieces, but is reconstituted by his wife/sister, Isis. But she cannot fine the phallus, so she replaces it with a wooden one. It is with this wooden phallus that Osiris impregnates Isis, who gives birth to their son Horus. The creativity following the dismemberment was thus of a spiritual nature.

June 11: * Peace comes when we are free from wanting to dominate people or things, or even our own soul. Our superficial motives can't destroy us if we're aware of the love we find in the ground of being. But a lifetime of isolation from ordinary human interaction and conflicts must finally be paid for. We must acknowledge our dependence on others and on "the other." Without that, we might easily succumb to despair which would deny the very existence of "something else." Carl Jung said the worst thing an analyst could do for his patients is try to take away their neurotic suffering on the surface and thus steal the one thing that could lead them to greater consciousness of the motives in their "ground of being."

June 12: * Electronic Data Systems of Plano, founded by free-trade opponent Ross Perot, announced last year a layoff of 5200. The company is among those that are sending white collar jobs to Chennai, India. Others are Verizon, Bank of America, Hewlett-Packard, Citibank, Visa, and MasterCard. The number of jobs lost to this phenomenon has surpassed a million, and Labor Dept. estimates the ultimate number at 14 million. Microsoft announced it would pay out $30 billion in stock dividends, but it didn't bring up the controversial news that it has twice as many employees in India as it did six months before. Microsoft employs nearly 2,000 workers in India, double the 970 number it previously acknowledged, as shown in internal company documents obtained by Washington Alliance of Technology Workers. There's no turning back from this trend. But we can stop giving tax breaks to corporations that have sham headquarters in the Caribbean and send their white collar jobs to India, although the trend is a boon to India's workers.

The most surprising news of the report on Microsoft is that the jobs going overseas are core development jobs, not just computer programming. "What is different is that Microsoft is a software development and not just a software services company," says Ron Hira, Assistant Prof. of Public Policy at the Rochester Institute of Technology. "That means that even development, supposedly the high level work that is supposed to remain in the U.S., is moving offshore." Hira points out that Microsoft has almost no competition and is generating record profits to the point where they have billions of dollars in cash. "It is one more indication that offshoring is driven to help executives and shareholders," Hira says.

June 13: * An American Indian myth says a certain tribe believed that when they arrived at the heavenly gates, the Great Hunter would ask one question before they could enter the happy hunting ground: "How many people are happier because you were born?"

June 14: * Our symbols teacher used to say that when we have a dream with one unrealistic element (like a purple cow), that is the aspect that expresses something significant, the thing our unconscious is trying to make us notice. We should spend some time trying to figure out why this image presented itself, and what it means to us.

* Andean potato farmers depend on the clarity of the Pleiades star cluster in June to determine the dates for planting their crop several months later. But Benjamin Orlov's research has revealed that the farmers are right. Invisible high-altitude cirrus clouds in June partially obscure the view of the Pleiades and also forecast an El Niño year, which is linked to low rainfall several months later.

* Ancient customs often reveal a nugget of truth. Ecuadorean farmers harvest their roof thatching reed in daylight when there is a full moon. Research has shown that photosensitive insects pests emerge in bright light and infest the reed, which then become a problem for inhabitants of the house.

June 15: * There were two prophets named Isaiah. The first (c. 740-700 B.C.) thought the young King Hezekiah was to be the Messiah. The second, who lived two centuries later (c. 545-518 B.C.) and wrote c. 539 B.C. in the period of the return of the Jews from exile in Babylon, apparently thought the Messiah was Persian King Cyrus the Great, who had overthrown the Medes in 550, conquered Anatolia by 546, and took over Babylon in 539. (The priest Ezra, who lived a century after the second Isaiah, agreed.) The second Isaiah called Cyrus "the anointed of Yahweh," but actually, Cyrus, a follower of Ahura Mazda, worshipped Marduk, god of Babylon, while he was there. Cyrus respected the local gods wherever he went and saw the similarity of gods in every culture.

June 16: * On June 16, 1933, President Roosevelt opened his New Deal recovery program, signing bank, rail, and industry bills and initiating farm aid, ushering in a new era of sharing in this country.

It's impossible to share without receiving. By giving work, time, talents, even positive thoughts, we feel satisfaction, happiness, and inner peace. When we give, our days are rich and life has meaning.

June 17: * Balthasar Gracián, a Spanish Jesuit priest, wrote *The Art of Worldly Wisdom* in 1637. Joseph Jacobs translated them. Wisdom ought to be timeless; some of Balthasar's is not. His advice might work for a CEO like The Donald, but is it wisdom? Balthasar comes across a trifle on the arrogant side, not the first priest I could say that about. I frankly think he should have spent more time eating raspberry tarts. Balthasar, in his own words: [*Mine are in brackets.*]

1. Be common in nothing. [*Neurotics believe they have to be perfect, because they don't know it's okay that they're only average.*]

2. Make people depend on you. [*This is manipulation.*]

3. Post yourself in the center of things. [*Oh sure, we all love a show-off. What's the matter with carrying a spear, being in the chorus, or hauling scenery and letting someone else be the star?*]

4. The shortest path to greatness is along with others. [*No, it's service to others.*]

5. Do not take payment in politeness. [*And why not, pray tell?*]

6. Make yourself sought after. [*Manipulation. And shallow.*]

7. Know how to get your price for things. [*What's the matter with not setting a price?*]

8. Set difficult tasks for those under you. [*That's right...whup 'em if they don't work harder.*]

Which reminds me of a great book called *Gil Blas*, a satire which pokes gentle fun at the Spanish Inquisition priests.

June 18: G..W. Bush ended his initial term as the first President since Herbert Hoover to oversee a net loss in employment. Of President Bush's economic policies, columnist Bob Herbert wrote: "[He] has behaved like a profligate parent who spends every dollar the family has accumulated, mortgages everything the family owns and maxes out every credit card he can get his hands on."

June 19: * On this date in 1865 General Gordon Granger landed on Galveston Island and told the slaves something they hadn't known before: that they weren't slaves at all! They were free. Thereafter, the black community has celebrated "Juneteenth" as Emancipation Day, even though it isn't the day that Lincoln signed the Emancipation Proclamation, or the day the War Between the States ended. After all, you're not free until you know you're free.

June 20: * From childhood, we're led to believe we must carry out our actions in a material way and have "dominion" over what we survey. We're encouraged to think our importance depends upon the possession of *things*. So power and wealth become the essence of life. But the more we consolidate our material dominion, identifying it as the meaning of our life, the more we lose the capacity for spiritual creation. It is necessary to experience first-hand how useless possession of *things* can be to satisfy the needs of the soul.

June 21: * From *Awareness* by Anthony de Mello: "You keep insisting I feel good because the world is right! Wrong! The world is right because I feel good. That's what the mystics are saying."

June 22: * The image of spinning abounds in antiquity. The Germanic Frigga spun clouds. Rumpelstiltskin spun straw into gold. Native American Spider Woman wove the four directions. In Japan, Amaterasu spun and wove sunbeams. In Egypt, Neith wove the world from her heavenly shuttle. The Greek Fates, Clotho, Lachesis, and Atropos, spun, measured, and cut the threads of human destiny.

June 23: * Surveys have found that ten percent of Icelanders believe in elves. Eighty percent say they won't totally rule them out. There is a seer in Reykjavik named Erla Stefansdottir who has seen elves since she was a child. She declared the village of Hafnarfjordur the capital of the elves in Iceland, and now Sigurbjorg Karlsdottir gives guided tours of the town. Stefansdottir says there are many types of elves and several types of gnomes and dwarfs.

June 24: * Author Sononfu Somé was raised among the Dagara people in rural a village in Burkina Faso, West Africa, where community and ritual are at the center of life. It literally takes a village to raise a child, even to name one, which is accomplished in a ritual before the baby is born. Sononfu's name means "keeper of the rituals." When couples decide to become parents, they are sent on a journey to heal their emotional wounds so they won't inflict them on the child. They go to the place where they were born and bring back some soil as a way of settling anything that is unresolved from their childhood. It is amazing how returning to a childhood home demystifies the past and frees us from it.

June 25: * Reuben Welch, quoted in *The Body Broken* by Robert Benson: "Sure, people need Jesus, but most of the time, what they really need is for someone to be Jesus to them."

* Revelation: All our battles are solitary ones. All our triumphs are group efforts. The noble times in our lives are our overcomings with a good grace.

June 26: * Power is an insidious drug. We were brought up on power, as were our parents and grandparents. We use power even when we don't know we're using it, even when we intend to do good. But we don't know another person's destiny. If we persist with our power tactics, we're going to destroy the earth. We don't have much time left in which to evolve. We're either going to have to make that leap in consciousness are we aren't going to be here. Power is no longer going to work, except to destroy.

We are often presented with an opportune moment to evolve, a "cubic centimeter of chance," when time is crucial to move instantly without conscious premeditation. This is the principle of economy of *means*, when very slight, deft movements at just the right time and place can have enormous consequences. When that opportunity comes, with just the slightest gesture in the right direction, all sorts of actions and results may be brought into being.

June 27: * Grace is the gift of Love. Love encourages us to continue discovering our potential and provides us with support to go beyond what we believe we are capable of doing. With Grace we can do more. It is the nature of Love to give and provide. Grace is our assurance that no matter what happens, we're not alone. Love supports us though every experience. Grace is magic.

Jung uses the word Love as "something superior to the individual, a unified and undivided whole." He said that man, being a part, cannot grasp the whole. "He is at its mercy. He may assent to it, or rebel against it; but he is always caught up by it and enclosed within it. He is dependent upon it and sustained by it." He says that man can try to name love and still he will involve himself in endless self-deceptions. "If he possesses a grain of wisdom, he will lay down his arms and name the unknown by the more unknown, "*ignotum per ignotius*"—that is, by the name of God."

June 28: * In his Eighteenth century *Commentaries on the Laws of England*, British scholar Sir William Blackstone described the legal conecpt of the *femme couverte* thus: "The very being of legal existence of the woman is suspended during the marriage, or at least is incorporated and consolidated into that of the husband, under whose wing, protection and cover she performs everything."

June 29: * Joan Acocella, in a *New Yorker* article entitled "Blocked," explores the reasons for writer's block. One is, paradoxically, great praise. (Cyril Connolly once said, "What the gods wish to destroy, they first call promising.") Another, according to Elizabeth Hardwick, is just the passing of youth. She says, "I don't think getting older is good for the creative process." Writers sometimes simply outlive their material. In 1960 Harper Lee published *To Kill a Mockingbird* which won the Pulitzer Prize. She was thirty-four. She has been working on another novel ever since. She is now seventy-nine.

June 30: * I have a special reverence for trees. A walk in the woods evokes immediate serenity. Trees seem stable, serene, even wise. Seneca once described in a letter something we've probably all felt:

"When you find yourself in a grove of exceptionally tall, old trees, whose interlocking boughs mysteriously shut out the view of the sky, the great height of the forest and the secrecy of the place together with a sense of awe before the dense impenetrable shades will awaken in you the belief in a god."

July:

July 1: * It takes discipline to have faith. But on morning walks Nature makes me realize I do have faith. Everywhere I see things I expect to see. A new day dawns as I knew it would; life springs up without anyone's effort. Nature reminds me to have faith—a knowing without asking, a calmness and trust. My faith includes accepting miracles without trying to explain them. Each day we accept miracles without looking for explanations. We live in a world of magic.

* Teilhard de Chardin: "I submit that the tension between science and faith should be resolved, not in terms either of elimination or duality, but in terms of synthesis."

July 2: * In the Texas Panhandle, we prize our trees. We love the fruit trees, of course, and the shade trees, but we also like the hardy junipers that do especially well there. On this date in 2003, *USA Today* ran an article that must have distressed any number of people there. It was about Bush's "Healthy Forest Initiative," which calls for thinning 190 *million* acres of forest land, harvesting old-growth trees deep in forests, far from communities affected by forest fires. It said, "There are only about 1.9 million acres of private and federal forest land—1% of the Bush's Administration's estimate—that are both at high risk of fire and close enough...to ignite homes."

The people of Northwest Texas are staunchly conservative, but they can only see this move as what it is: a gift to the logging industry. How, I wonder, does this differ from the dangerous deforestation of the Amazon rain forest?

July 3: * The symptoms of a loss of faith on the personal level are: an inability to make progress, the loss of a relationship, the loss of interest in things one previously found interesting, the loss of meaning of values and personal codes of conduct, lack of concern for the consequences of one's rash acts.

* In the Sahara Desert, there is a town named Tidikelt, which did not receive a drop of rain for ten years.

* Spain literally means "the land of rabbits."

* St. Paul, Minnesota was originally called Pigs Eye after Pierre

"Pig's Eye" Parrant, who set up the first business there.

July 4: * When our children were young, we liked to go camping. In the evening, with the star canopy overhead, as we sat around the campfire watching the flames in a sort of hypnotic state, their dad would say, "There's something magical about a fire. Man has been sitting like this, watching a fire, for thousands of years." He said it as if it were a new revelation, even though he said the same thing every time. We used to roll our eyes and snicker, because we knew his spiel by heart, but at the same time, it was comforting, because it was true. And maybe he did indeed feel that it was a new magical revelation every time.

Sir Laurens van der Post once overheard two students. One said, "What is fire?" and the other answered, "It is energy." Van der Post thought, "Dear Heaven, can we be as intellectual as all that? Surely fire is light in the dark...warmth against the cold...security against the...things that prowl by night. People no longer see the sun as a great source of light but as gasses and sunspots. The great sun-within-themselves, the interaction between what goes on in the universe and themselves, is cut off.... Fire is just energy to us."

How I wish I could recapture the magic of those nights under stars, gazing into the crackling fire that connects me with my own past, and with humankind since our early beginnings.

July 5: * The symptoms of a loss of faith on the collective level are: a breakdown of cultural values, the failure of communally-held social conventions, increased cultural expression of more primitive behavior as immediate gratification, greed, rage. Edward F. Edinger said, "Meaning is lost....Primitive and atavistic elements are reactivated. Differentiated values disappear and are replaced by the elemental motivations of power and pleasure....With the loss of awareness of a transpersonal reality (God), the inner and outer anarchies of competing personal desires take over."

July 6: * Worrisome: George W. Bush judicial nominee James Leon Holmes said: "The wife is to subordinate herself to her husband ... to place herself under the authority of the man."

Bush judicial nominee William Pryor argued that the Violence

Against Women Act was unconstitutional. Bush judicial nominee Carolyn Kuhl ruled against a woman who claimed her privacy had been violated by a doctor who allowed a drug salesman to hang out in the room with them—and laugh at her—while the doctor examined her breasts. Bush judicial nominee Priscilla Owen consistently ruled to restrict access to abortion without parental consent. George Bush described his own wife as "the lump in the bed next to me."

*Actually, Laura Bush is a national treasure. If every culture needs its Virgin Mary, then Laura Bush is ours. A CNN program about her and about Cheney said Laura saved George from self-destruction by threatening to leave him if he didn't stop drinking. Lynn Cheney saved Dick, who didn't plan to continue his education, by telling him that she wouldn't marry him if he didn't go to school.

History will rank our leaders, *and* their wives. Democratic Senator Minority Leader Harry Reid said in a candid *New Yorker* interview, "I have served three Republican Presidents. President Reagan—I cared a great deal for him, and he got most of what he wanted. If you disagreed with him, he did not hold it against you. President Bush Number One is such a nice person. Some of my most prized possessions are the three letters he wrote me. But this President [Bush] is totally different. He takes after his mother. It's either his way or no way. It's very, very difficult."

July 7: * Addiction isn't just escape from something intolerable. It's based on the search for *perfection*, an Absolute. The addict's search for meaning in life and nourishment for the hungry soul begins with the yearning to belong. In our society, we believe that unless we're perfect, we don't belong. But the reality is that our limitations are crucial to who we are. They make us human.

During the 80s there was a wonderful guitarist, Stanley Jordan, who invented a "tapping" technique so that he could play a melody with his left hand, which usually holds down the frets. A Princeton graduate, he gave up performing because he was a perfectionist. That reminds me of Juan Rulfo, considered Mexico's greatest novelist. He was such a perfectionist that very little of his writing was ever published. Someone took his manuscript of *Pedro Paramo* out of the waste basket, or the world would never have known about his writing genius.

How many creative gifts has the world lost because man fails to realize he can never be perfect?

Another fantastic guitarist was a Manouche gypsy: Django Reinhardt, born in 1910 in a caravan on the road in Belgium. When he was twelve he got a bastardized banjo-guitar and learned how to play it from a Gitan virtuoso. He developed a stiff-armed, elbow-dependent technique that eventually led him to create the Quintet of the Hot Club of France. Usually the group included Django on lead guitar, Django's brother Nin-Nin on one rhythm guitar and the ganster-Gypsy Baro Ferret on another, Louis Vola on bass, and Stephane Grappelli on violin. Django and Stephane had both first heard American jazz in 1931: Louis Armstrong in particular. The experience had changed both their lives. Django played a Selmer with a small sounding hole. The group made some recordings in the thirties that are the sourve of the world's Djangomania. It was only after his death in 1953 that people began to imitate his music.

July 8: * The loss of faith is a subjective, individual experience of a collective dilemma. Either one's psychic potential can be contained in the collective myth or it cannot. For Jung, the individual loss of faith or meaning is already a sign of cultural distress. He says: "...there is bound to be a considerable number of individuals who are possessed by archetypes of a numinous nature that force their way to the surface in order to form new dominants." He describes two instances in which a new conscious dominant arose at the collective level—Buddhism and Christianity. In both cases the principle holds true. Buddhism grew naturally out of ancient Hinduism and exists now side by side with competing practices. With Christianity, the case is more complicated. Hebrew faith that was the soil of Christian inspiration dated back to the late Bronze Age. More accurately, modern Judaism and Christianity grew from the same historical crisis of faith in the early Hebrew religion.

July 9: * An early "threnody (lamentation for the dead) for the lost god" occurs in an account by Plutarch, who tells a tale about a sailing vessel that comes upon the Echinades Islands and everyone on board hears a voice instructing them to announce that "great Pan is dead." When they passed by Palodes, the pilot calls out, "Great

Pan is dead!" Plutarch reports that the Roman emperor Tiberius was so distressed by the story that he ordered an investigation concerning the god Pan.

This announcement about the death of Pan is a distant echo of Nietzsche's "death of God" announcement in *Thus Spake Zarathustra.* He meant that we're living in a cultural context in which we're all infected with the same collective dilemma. Science has robbed us of our simple faith. Jung once said that at the bottom of all his patients' problems: "There has not been one whose problem in the last resort was not that of finding a religious outlook on life." He claimed that every one of his patients fell ill because he had lost what the living religions of every age have provided for their followers, and that none of his patients were ever healed unless they regained their religious outlook.

July 10: * Dante says of Lucifer's fall from Heaven: "...he fell anon,/ Unripe, because he would not wait for light...." The "original sin" from which his disobedience sprang was haste; in Dante's estimation, the knowledge of evil was not in itself forbidden. "I want what I want, and I want it *now.*" Haste is born with the ego's consciousness of time. When a child begins to hurry after a conscious goal, innocence is left behind. Waiting is the life-long task of discriminating, patience from cowardice and inertia, creative movement from impatient driving toward a goal. We are cast out of Eden because of the frenetic hurry which dominates our lives.

July 11: * According to Shakespeare's *King Lear*, the four proper occupations of old age are: *prayer*, which is the rooting of the attention in the ground of being; *song*, which is the expression of spontaneous joy in the harmony of the chaos; the *"telling of old tales,"* which among all tribal societies is the supreme function of the old, who pass on the wisdom of the ancestors through the symbol, through the understanding of the dreams of the race that their long experience has taught them; and *laughter*—the laughter of pure delight in beauty.

These four things are activities *without purpose*; any one of them is immediately killed by any hint of striving for achievement.

Lear finishes this speech with the final responsibility of each person's life: "And take upon's the mystery of things, as if we were God's spies."

July 12: * The Goddess of the Hearth in ancient Greece was Hestia, a virgin. Her Roman name was Vesta, and the sacred hearth fire of the city was constantly tended by the Vestal Virgins. The symbol of the holy prostitute has a special meaning unrelated to our present understanding of the word "virgin." Originally the word meant "she who is one-in-herself." Philo of Alexandria said that when a virgin lay with a man she became a woman, but when God had intercourse with the soul, the woman became a virgin again. Esther Harding has said that woman must do the hardest thing of all for the feminine psyche, which is to allow herself to love someone with her whole being from whom she knows she can expect no return, no fruition.

July 13: * We have probably all experienced times in which we realize that others no longer understand us. But this, far from being a negative fact, is a sign of our emancipation. If we were always to be understood, it would mean that we were speaking the language of others, a collective language. But is our attitude and ideas are original, we can no longer be understood.

July 14: * In the *Phaedrus*, Plato says that "the greatest boons come to us through madness, which is granted as a divine gift." Throughout the Greek world, madness is the "matrix of wisdom."

Whatever progress we may make in our psychological development, it doesn't take much to return to an instinctual level—as my friend Peggy Ingram says, the lizard brain. This means not only biological impulses, but also thoughtless adherence to unconscious convictions and opinions so that we react automatically instead of logically. Jung says, "The insinuations of the anima, the mouthpiece of the unconscious, can utterly destroy a man."

July 15: * Abraham Lincoln said: "I study to prepare myself and when my time comes, perhaps I will be ready."

* From the Gospel of Phillip: "You must awaken while in this body, for everything exists in it: resurrect in this life.".

July 16: * It is easier to be negative than positive, easier to be angry than forgiving, because to forgive, we must first get pride out of the way. Redirecting a thought pattern is like breaking up housekeeping and starting out for a new land. Nothing happens to us that did not first happen in our minds. As we think, so we are.

Some people believe that even though we may not want it to be, our every thought is a prayer. All power of heaven is directed toward its manifestation. Obviously not every thought springs into manifestation, but every thought makes its mark, and enough marks make a picture, which is the manifestation. A thought held in mind without being opposed by contrary thoughts is bound to come forth.

Our degree of happiness is gauged by the extent to which we express our potential: what we would most like to do or be. It isn't what seems most glamorous or exciting, or what someone else says we should do, or what is most profitable or high-profile. It's what gives us the greatest sense of satisfaction.

All our energy must go undivided toward a vision of success. We can't waste a minute on thoughts of failure or obstacles. We focus on what we want to accomplish. We can do infinitely more than we may have originally thought. Instead of seeing the difficulties in a situation, we must choose to see the potential for good.

July 17: * If J. M. Barrie, creator of *Peter Pan*, were living today, he would probably be treated as harshly as Michael Jackson. Barrie frequented playgrounds and collected young boys. But his biographer, Andrew Birkin, says that Barrie was "a lover of childhood, but was not in any sexual sense the pedophile that some claim him to have been." His plan was to escape to childhood himself. Carl Jung called this type of person *puer aeternus* (forever the boy), and we've all known men like this. Another example of boy-man was St. Exupery, who wrote *The Little Prince*. The idea of flying around—ungrounded, as Jung would say—is similar in both their fantasies. But Barrie is not alone in his desire to escape to Neverland. Consider Lewis Carroll or Edward Lear. I see similarities between these men and Jackson, whose great tragedy may have been in living in the wrong century.

July 18: * We have to discover the magnificent consciousness in matter and thus in our own bodies. We are capable of seeing the light in a rose bush, of feeling the energy in a tree. We are born to live in the love that permeates all of life.

Selene, Goddess of the Moon, rose from an obscure cave and set into the same cave. She was characterized by her unsurpassed beauty, her eye which saw all things happening below, her rule of menstruation, the orderly rhythm of female instinct, her relation with epilepsy and healing, the veil that kept her partly hidden and indirect, the torch she carried and her light-bestowing diadem.

For his conquest of the moon, Pan had to disguise his black and hairy parts with white fleece. By becoming white, Pan turns reflective. So Pan, by becoming like Selene, is already connected with her. Are we so different?

July 19: * It's very rare that we focus on what we want to create for *its own sake*. Robert Frost said, "All great things are done for their own sake." When we see our visions in this way, it creates a subtle but profound shift. This is when "hidden hands" begin to help, and doors open that we could hardly have imagined.

* There are no natural lakes in the state of Ohio, every one is manmade.

* The smallest island with country status is Pitcairn in Polynesia, at just 1.75 sq. miles/4,53 sq. km.

July 20: * The Romans had two words to signify divine presences: *deus*, akin to the Sanskrit *deva*, which indicates a being with defined personality; hence, "god"; and *numen,* which we Westerners find hard to translate because it is a concept that we don't have. That is, we of western European heritage don't have it, inasmuch as we have borrowed our religious beliefs from the Levant, or Middle East. Certainly Native Americans have the concept, and it is also found in the South Pacific and in Asia. And from my study of epics, I found that among peasants in Finland, Slavic Russia, Lithuania and other Baltic states, and in the Balkan countries like Albania, Bulgaria, Croatia, Romania, Serbia, Slovenia, and even Greece, these concepts are very real to this day. The root from which the term is derived means "nod." It means a sort of immanent magical force emanating from certain phenomena. In other words, the *numen* within a thing is its acknowledgement of you.

Now, thinking back to my childhood, I can understand. As a young child, I felt great respect for everything I used, maybe a table, for instance. If I touched the table on one side, I might then feel obliged to touch it on the other side, so something in its nature wouldn't feel slighted. A child feels great kinship with everything around her. Memory of these beliefs remains strong after these many years, which leads me to wonder if they were transferred in my DNA from my animistic ancestors.

In Roman times, the most influential *numina* were in the home. The *penates* were (and *still are* in northeastern Europe!) numina of the larder. The *lares* were—*and are*—numina of household effects. The table I mentioned might have been considered host to a *lare.*

July 21: * We have a wild side, an inheritance from our primitive brain parts. All people in the world are not at the same stage of development, either. Some still reside in that earlier brain, at least part of the time. It's a temptation for any intelligent person to ignore or try to kill off the primitive, emotive, appetitive self, but even if we could, it would be a disastrous mistake. It is as dangerous to ignore the existence of the irrational as it is to try to kill it off. Yet the more cultured a person is, the more "intelligent," the more repressed, the more obsessed with order, the more he needs some method for channeling the primitive impulses he has worked so hard to subdue. Otherwise, those powerful old forces will mass and strengthen until they are violent enough to break free, more violent for the delay, often strong enough to sweep away the will entirely. On the personal level, we have seen disastrous results to marriage when one of the partners has a "mid-life crisis."

We have seen this on a grand scale in the Nazi era of the orderly Germans, where unreasoning hate caused the unimaginable horror of the holocaust, and in the old Roman era, when the well-organized Romans, once so tolerant of foreign religions, threw Christians to the lions. We see it on a smaller scale in our own lives, as for an extreme example, when a middle-aged man, meticulous to a fault in his duty to work and family, suddenly breaks his traces and completely irrationally abandons all for a life of hedonism. Even if we haven't experienced a full-blown "mid-life crisis," if we examine our lives, we can find traces of such behavior, all because we believed that we could deny our fundamental primitive humanity.

July 22: * There's a difference between judgment and discernment. Judgment connotes condemnation, or placing blame. But pointing fingers seldom solves problems. Bill likes to say of our household, "We live in a no-fault world." Lao Tzu said, "The good man does not seek culprits, he seeks solutions."

July 23: * One way to recognize "magic" is to acknowledge the various parts of the psyche. James Hillman writes that the reason our time has become so godless and profane is that we lack all knowledge of the unconscious psyche, and we pursue the "cult" of consciousness to the exclusion of all else. He quotes Jung: "*Our true religion is a monotheism of consciousness, a possession by it,* coupled with a fanatical denial of the existence of fragmentary autonomous systems." (italics Hillman's)

When the dominant vision that holds a period of culture together cracks, consciousness regresses into earlier modes, seeking sources not only for survival but also for revival—*there's an example of the past pressed up against the present again.* ("Renaissance" would be a senseless word without the implied death out of which the rebirth comes.) Our culture shows two alternate paths for the earlier modes: Hellenism (representing multiplicity, as in the various gods of Greek myth) and Hebrewism, (representing unity, or Yaweh—Yahweh). Europeans have drifted and vacillated between the two. At the times of the Renaissance and Reformation, southern Europe returned to Hellenism, while northern Europe returned to Hebrewism.

Hebrewism, reconfirming the monotheism of ego-consciousness, suits a culture when the consciousness senses that its survival is best served by an archetypal pattern of heroism and individualism, represented by the early image of Christ, which was compounded with the military god Mithra who preceded him. Plutarch's (ca. 46-120 C.E.) famous report (in "On the Failure of the Oracles") that "the Great God Pan is dead" coincides with the ascension of Christianity, for Constantine's conversion to Christianity turned the tide against classical polytheism and for a while buried the sense of multiplicity from the European psyche. (There are legends about the irreconcilable conflict between Christ and Pan—a conflict that continues to rage today in the minds of fundamentalists, since the Devil which they take literally, with his horns and hooves, is none other than a fundamentalist version of Great Pan from Greek myth.)

Gradually myths that guided human behavior since early human history resurfaced, for they're never far from conscious awareness. Later, in the Reformation, Hebrewism reinserted itself, inspired by the fantasy of unified heroic strength like Siegfried's or Sir Gawain's.

The Greek myth of polytheism serves less specifically as a religion and more generally as a psychology, for as it turns out, the soul or psyche is very much a variety of parts, each of which may "rule" at various moments in our lives. The early Catholic Church, which attempted to stamp out everything different from itself, labeled long-held myths as evils from which the supplicant must be purged. But there is no need for deliverance from evil if the thing that is different isn't imagined to be evil in the first place.

During the last two centuries, the priesthood's grip on Western thinking has weakened to allow investigation of the myths that are part of our psychic heritage. There would have been no investigation if there had been no need, if what the church offered satisfied the soul. What was missing? What had we left behind? What was there to fear, as the early church fathers warned? (*Hmm: Was it partly their sexual repression, mandated by the church, that sometimes broke its bonds and surfaced in unspeakable acts against those in their charge who were weaker and unlikely to question their authority?)* Jung labeled it the Shadow: all the buried parts of ourselves that we refuse to acknowledge, that at times make us do things we had no conscious intention of doing. (Didn't Saint Paul speak of doing the very things he hadn't intended to do?) Turns out we're much more complicated than anyone ever dreamed. For centuries we searched the heavens and plumbed the earth for secrets and left out the investigation of ourself, the biggest mystery of all.

The psyche in crisis has many fantasies. Hellenism's many and Hebrewism's one aren't the only paths out of the psyche's pathological dilemma. Some escape into futurism and technology; others turn to Eastern thought, delving inward; others go primitive and natural. Some combine a variety of these approaches to integrate the parts of their complicated psyches, or, to use Abraham Maslow's term, to "self-actualize." Self-discovery, it turns out, is the adventure of a lifetime, leading ultimately to confrontations with *magic*.

July 24: * Basques, the oldest surviving ethnic group in Europe, remain a mystery. No one knows where they came from, and despite the fact that they are a nation without a country, Basques have had a disproportionate impact on world history. For example, it was the Basques who cut down Roland and the rest of Charlemagne's rear guard at Roncesvalles; and a Basque, St. Ignatius Loyola, founded the Jesuits. Primarily, they live in the area of the Pyrenees, but there are a few Basque names among Celtic populations in Great Britain.

July 25: * In 1789, the *HMS Lady Julian* left England bound for Australia's New South Wales. Its cargo: 237 women, most of them young petty criminals, who proved themselves to be resourceful but "disorderly girls." Their story is told by Siân Rees in a book titled *The Floating Brothel*.

* In Kentucky, every citizen is required to have a bath at least once a year.

July 26: * Every culture has its own demons. The Slavs have a nightmare demon, *Serpolnica*, a female. Among the Slavic Wends, the nightmare demon is *Murawa*. If you call him by his name, he will leave. Wood ghosts often appear as nightmare demons, as for example, the Celtic *Dusii* (first mentioned by Augustinus and characterized as nightmare demons lying in wait for women) and the Italic Silvanus and Faunus. Veckenstedt, in his *Lithuanian Myths*, speaks of the Lithuanian *Medine*, or forest woman: "...whoever goes through the wood,...the Medine forces him to struggle with her; should he be victorious, he is richly rewarded, but if he is defeated, she devours him."

He describes small nightmare demons with long grey beards called *Cauci*, who, at full moon, glide into the room to throttle the sleeper. In German superstition, you must call the demon by his name to capture and get him in your power, like: Rumplestiltskin, but there are others. If you know the name of a *Doggi*—nightmare spectre—or of a *Fanken*, you have him in your power. For protection against witches in the form of animals, to force them to resume their human form, they must be called three times by their Christian name. The witches then usually appear naked.

The blessing that a nightmare demon confers may consist in the communication of useful secrets or in the granting of good health. Blessing, doing good, and being of service, is developed to an exceptional degree in the Germanic domestic spirits or *familiars* (*spiritus familiares*) who are at the same time nightmare demons. The connection between the name of Mephistopheles and Ophelis-Epophelis ("helper, benefactor") becomes clear since he was one of those useful domestic spirits, according to the old Faust legend.

Superstitious people alter the names of frightening demons for fear the demons may cause mischief if called by their correct names.

The malicious *kobolds*, according to the Homeric pottery-blessing, create mischief in the potter's oven by wrecking the vessels. Even today, reports of the modern Greek demon, the *Laboma*, lives on in the beliefs of the shepherds of Parnassus. According to B. Schmidt: "This being is in the habit of mounting goats in the form of a he-goat and bringing about their sudden death. Many shepherds from the Parnassus claim to have been eye-witnesses of this and say that the animals are seized by excruciating pains during copulation with the demon...." The corycic grotto, which was already dedicated to Pan and to the nymphs in ancient times, is still a secure place of refuge for the shepherds of Parnassus and their flocks, because Pan was considered as an attacker like the present day demon *Laboma*, and they are probably the same.

The goat-shaped *Koutsodaimnoas* of modern Greeks probably corresponds to the ancient Greek Pan. The old Indian nightmare demons, the *Gandharves* and *Rakshas*, show a remarkable similarity to Pan, Faunus, Silvanus, and the satyrs. They abide in dark places and can driving women into a frenzy. Their female counterparts are the *Apsaras*, who are comparable to elves, nymphs, and sirens.

July 27: * James Prosek, an artist and writer whom I heard on NPR, traveled the world in search of rare trout to paint, then settled two doors down from his boyhood home in Easton, Conn. He still fishes in the same pond he fished as a child, and he paints in an 1850 one-room schoolhouse that he has been drawn to all his life. When he was a schoolboy, a teacher interrupted class to let students watch a truck roll by carrying the old building, which was being moved across town. When he came home that day, he saw it had been relocated to his street. He said, "I almost felt like a celebrity." In 1991, a house was built around the schoolhouse, and a few years later Prosek bought it. His studio is in the schoolhouse, which he says he tries to make sound smaller than it is because, "I want it to be a humble space. *Humility is a big part of being open and receptive to everything you see. Part of being a good observer is to know you don't know anything.*" He's very wise for a person of 29

July 28: * The alphabet is older by about three centuries than we thought—and first appeared in a different country than what we thought, according to David Sachs in *Language Visible* (Broadway Books, 2004). Yale U. Egyptologist John C. Darnell found carved inscriptions along an ancient Egyptian desert road that placed the invention of the alphabet around 2000 B.C. Around 1000 B.C. this "ancestor" produced a prime descendant: the Phoenician alphabet, which is the "great-grandmother" of many Roman letters used in about 100 languages worldwide today. The letters V and J are relative newcomers, having been accepted just two centuries ago. Classical Latin had no J sound. Julius Caesar was actually Iulius.

July 29: * In 1904 Max Weber wrote his most important work and a founding text of an emerging field of sociology: *The Protestant Ethic and the Spirit of Capitalism.* Weber posed the question: why did modern capitalism come into being in a particular region (northern Europe) at a particular time (the seventeenth century) even though the greed for gold is as old as the history of man? We all, whatever our occupation, accept the notion that our jobs ought to be more than just a way to sustain ourselves. We acknowledge working to be our duty. Now, according to Weber, only a well-ordered bureaucracy is capable of supporting a modern technological society. The incoherence of modern life became his theme. He used the term "dis-enchantment" to describe the way that science and technology had displaced magical thinking. Rationality was king, but he thought that we all—rich and poor, owners and workers—live lives of quiet desperation. Although he wrote this cultural history a century ago, it has foretold many developments since. Most recently, the triumph of Wal-Mart, the demise of the family farm, the flow of blue-collar jobs across the Rio Grande and white-collar jobs to Bangalore are consistent with Weber's notions of "progress" and the futility of trying to resist it—or even wanting to resist it. He said, "When asceticism was carried out of monastic cells into everyday life and began to dominate worldly morality, it did its part in building the tremendous cosmos of the modern economic order. This order is now bound to the technical and economic conditions of machine production which today determine the lives of all the individuals who are born into this mechanism,...with irresistible force." Materialism has become, in his words, "an iron cage."

July 30: * In Scotland, a clootie well is a sacred place where people visit, requesting help or a cure, and leaving behind a piece of rag (clootie). It used to be at the beginning of May that people came, but now it happens all year round. It is a good idea not to disturb any rags one finds lying around.

The Shetland Islands' St. Kilda Island is the only island named after a saint that never existed.

July 31: * Scotland's "The Long Island" was, until the turn of the 20th Century, Britain's only island with two names: Lewis and Harris, part of the Outer Hebrides. Harris Tweed is in reality Lewis Tweed, because it was first manufactured in Harris. The Harris Tweed Authority was founded in 1909 and awards its famous "Orb Mark" only to those wool products made of 100 % virgin wool dyed, spun and finished in the Outer Hebrides and hand-woven by islanders on looms in their own homes. "Tweed is a 160-year-old misspelling of "tweel," meaning "twill."

*The Eisenhower interstate system requires that one-mile in every five must be straight. These straight sections are usable as airstrips in times of war or other emergencies.

* Thomas Aquinas (1225-74) described the Seven Deadly Sins as sloth, gluttony, lust, anger, pride, envy and greed. But in a recent BBC poll, Brits, retaining only greed from the original seven, ranked cruelty, adultery, selfishness, dishonesty, bigotry and hypocrisy as worse sins. I would rank greed as the granddaddy.

August

August 1: * The Celtic holiday Lughnasa, Lammas Day, was August 1. The name is derived from the Old English *hlafmaesse*, "the loaf mass," from the ancient tradition of offering neighbors bread made from the new season's wheat. The Celtic god Lugh presided over a harvest festival that lasted many days.

* Harriet Beecher Stowe: "Your little child is your only true democrat."

August 2: * In the past, nobody had heard of the term "dysfunctional family," although there were probably plenty of them. It was the family's duty to be happy, no matter what. In the dysfunctional family that pretended to be happy, the harmony and perfection that everyone feigned at the family dinner table was often absent, but nobody admitted the absence. Denial is fundamental in addictive families: denial of what's absent, the loving, happy family; and denial of that is present, a problem.

August 3: * The culture of ancient Egypt began in 3100 B.C. and survived for more than 2000 years. The Egyptians believed in life after death, as evidenced by their mummies and pyramids. After these millennia, the pyramids remain the oldest and most massive stone structures in the world. Many Egyptian cities had libraries containing thousands of papyrus scrolls, the most notable library in the ancient world being in Alexandria. Both women and men wore makeup, necklaces and bracelets and used perfume.Unlike modern Egyptians, women were entitled to many of the same rights as men. There are three novels by Naguib Mahfouz (caused to be translated into English by Jackie Onassis) that give us a picture of modern Egypt, or at least Egypt as it was in the Twentieth Century. They are called "The Cairo Trilogy." My favorite is the first, *Palace Walk.*

August 4: * Once we have become comfortable with the *anima* (feminine aspect), once it has been assimilated into our psyche, comes the leadership of the "wise old man." When the archetype of the Self appears in dreams in human form, the image is almost always of the same sex as the dreamer. The guide to the inner world is of the opposite sex; the *anima* in man or the *animus* in woman is the link between the personal world and the archetypal depths.

We must discover the "motive in the ground of our beseeching"—and let go of profit motives and the demand for results. In the feminine psyche, the hidden power and profit motives are the subtle desire to possess and manipulate those close to us, or else to be supported, even possessed, by the love of others so as to have protection from danger, loneliness, and responsibility. The unconscious in man has similar problems of jealousy and possessiveness, but on the whole his danger lies in the exercise of power in the outer world.

August 5: * Ariel, the "tricksy spirit" in Shakespeare's *The Tempest*, who is being held in bondage by Prospero, is an elusive image no words can capture. On the psychological level, Ariel is an unknown "something" in the unconscious that seems to urge us through dreams and synchronistic events—whenever we touch the realm of archetypes—toward greater consciousness. And when the time comes for the final "letting go" at the time of death, Ariel begins to urge the ego toward it by pressing for his freedom again. At the height of his success, Prospero must determine whether he dares honor his promise to Ariel to free him, and try to manage without the powers that he has built up over his lifetime. It is a moment of extreme danger: of embracing a hubris that brings total destruction.

So many leaders, past and present, make the mistake of believing that, once they have become powerful, they did it all by themselves and that they are larger than life. They have forgotten the promise, the bargain, "to free Ariel." William Blake calls this elusive image a joy: "He who bends to himself a joy/ Doth the winged life destroy;/ But he who kisses the joy as it flies/ Dwells in eternity's sunrise."

August 6: * The *New York Times* reported that according to IRS data, *for the first time in modern history*, Americans' overall income fell for two consecutive years, between 2000 and 2002. Reporter David Cay Johnston said that average individual income fell by 9.2 percent between 2000 and 2002. A study by the MIT Workplace Center found the average two-parent family spent 15 percent more time working in 2000 than in 1985 and that U.S. parents now work more hours than their counterparts in any other country of the world.

Another study by the Economic Policy Institute found that workers' real weekly and hourly earnings are lower now than they were in November 2001, when the recession officially ended. Earnings have fallen for six of the past seven months. Gas prices have risen for good, most analysts agree.

August 7: * A tendency toward the preservation of the past is childish, but it accompanies us throughout our lives, because it underlies a need for security that is never completely fulfilled.

* In 1724 a French law was enacted which said that all who assembled for Protestant worship, even in their homes, were liable for servitude for life, and their property would be confiscated. Another law condemned to death any Protestant minister exercising any religious function and also condemned to the galleys anyone who didn't report the minister. A third law demanded that physicians inform the Catholic church of the medical condition of anyone who might be dying or face the galleys themselves. A fourth law mandated the galleys and confiscation of goods of any Protestant who strengthened a dying relative in his religious beliefs.

August 8: * Anglo Saxons were a bloody lot, but they can't hold a candle to Scotsmen. It was a Scottish belief that when a man is murdered, his ghost lingers on until his normal life span has been completed. Clan chiefs, and later kings, routinely met a violent end. In 954, Malcolm I was killed in battle. Malcolm III (c.1031-c.1093) was killed in Alnwick, and Macbeth was killed by Malcolm III's men on August 15, 1057. Alexander III and his horse fell over a cliff in 1286. In 1286, Sir William Wallace led the resistance to English invaders under Edward I. He was taken to London, hanged on August 22, 1305, then drawn, beheaded, and quartered. James I was assassinated on February 20, 1437. A young James II was present at Edinburgh Castle when the sixth Earl of Douglas was murdered at the Black Dinner. James II personally murdered the eighth Earl in 1452 and was himself killed in the siege at Roxbrough on August 3, 1460. James III, fleeing from insurgents, fell from his horse. He called for a priest, and the man claiming to be one stabbed him in the heart. Mary, Queen of Scots, plotted for years against her cousin Elizabeth of England. It has long been speculated that Mary connived with the fourth Earl of Bothwell in the murder of her husband, Lord Darnley, in 1567. [My friend Olivia Orfield wrote a brilliant award-winning play, *Death Trap,* about that. It was published by Performance Publishing Company.] Three months later, Mary married Bothwell. But after another death plot, she herself was condemned to death. She was executed on February 8, 1587.

August 9: * When something bad happens, friends may say in consolation that as one door closes, another opens. Intellectually, I know it's true, but at the time, I often feel that one door has shut and I'm standing in a tiny vestibule by myself. Scientist Rupert Sheldrake talks about thinking of the past as pressed up against the present, and as potentially present everywhere. I have felt this. If I am standing in a figurative vestibule behind and before closed doors, before I step across the threshold to something else, it would be well to gather up what I've learned from the past and to tarry a while in that small space, however cramped, while I sort them over. Regardless of the circumstances, there are lessons to be brought forward.

August 10: * About the second part of that original statement above: Suppose the door closes on an old belief that I cannot in all conscience make myself embrace any longer. But where is the door opening to a new belief? This is the dilemma facing many since the middle of the last century. There are very few guides to help us grope toward an alternate, no matter how far afield we look. We are left to our own devices. There's no place to look except within.

But. My tendency is to drag everything along through life. Maybe it's my Scottish heritage. Edwin Muir, in his 1935 book, *Scottish Journey*, said, "I think it is possible that all Scots are illegitimate, Scotsmen being so [stingy] and Scotswomen so generous." But there comes a time when not everything will fit through the ever-narrowing doors. Besides, it gets wearying, carrying all that stuff.

As doors close and new ones open, it may appear we're leaving everything behind, but there's one constant we take along: Love. It guides us through endings, transforming fear into courage, doubt into self-confidence, sorrow into joy, uncertainly into anticipation. There is magic ahead, and divine laws support and bless us.

August 11: * A mathematician and logician, G. Spenser-Brown developed a new system of logic, which could be compared with a computer that gets caught in the self-referential paradox of the Cretan. The Cretan says, "All Cretans are liars." Clearly the Cretan must be referring to himself as well, but can he be speaking the truth? If so, then the statement, "All Cretans are liars," is true and therefore the statements that each individual Cretan makes are false. But if the statement is false, then all Cretans are not liars but speak the truth. But in this case, the statement must be true, and therefore the Cretan is a liar, in which case…." ad infinitim. Clearly the best a computer could do is to continue this endless loop, generating answers, Truth, Lie, Truth, Lie, or Yes, No, Yes, No…or 0,1,0,1,0… Spenser-Brown says that such a stable oscillation occurs both in computers and in biological systems and represents the generation of time, as the cyclic repetition and the continuous unfolding are set in opposition to each other. This is the logic of distinctions and dualities which is supposed to underlie the structure of the world.

August 12: * The idea from Isaiah, "I have called thee by thy name; thou art mine," also has a basis in the field of physics. Creation through the evolution of distinctions, categories, and contexts is also found in creation myths which equate the appearance of order with the act of naming. Names have an active quality that is able to produce order out of chaos. The act of naming creates distinctions so that the named stands out against the background and thereby establishes a movement of distinction.

In early religions, it was necessary to name the spirit or elemental to invoke its presence and bind it to the magician or priest's will. We see this in fairy tales such as Rumpelstiltskin, who lost his power over the princess when she guessed his name. In Egyptian times, to erase the name on a tomb was to remove a person from eternal life.

"Naming the Beast" is what writers and painters do when we bring to life the images of our unconscious. We are claiming parts of ourselves, making ourselves more whole.

It is this movement of meaning which pervades the universe of mind and matter, of consciousness and the body, and of the individual and society. A central creativity pervades everything.

August 13: * Some therapists help their clients, their partner, their family, trying to fulfill someone else's needs, having no idea how to fill their own because they have been the offspring of narcissistic parents. It may be that the whole plan of life is simple. What we have to do is follow the meaning in our life. We simply take up the tasks that are presented to us. Life will do its own thing. We don't have to worry about it or try to make things happen. "Whatever thy hand finds to do, do it with all thy might."

August 14: * When Victor Hugo wanted to know how *Les Misérables* was selling, he telegraphed his publisher: "?" To which the publisher responded: "!"

* Oh for solitude, the way one was solitary as a child. The necessary thing is solitude, great inner solitude.

August 15: * The Roman poet Martial (M. Valerius Martialis, fl. AD 80-AD 96), said, in a modern translation by Brendan Kennelly:

"What constitutes a happy life?/ Enough money to meet your needs/ steady work/ a comfortable fire / a clear distance from law / a minimum of city business /a peaceful mind and a healthy body / simple wisdom and firm friends / enjoyable dinners and plain living /nights free from care / a virtuous wife who's not a prude / enough sleep to make the darkness short / contentment with the life you have, / avoiding the sneer, the poisoned sigh; / no fear of death / and no desire to die."

August 16: * My priorities differ from Martial's. My happiness consists of: a simple life/ good health/ someone to love (I still love even when I'm left alone)/ meaningful work that justifies the space I take up on this earth/ fast friends who don't expect much/ a home/ a comfortable living/ trees and flowers that teach me about serenity

August 17: * As corporations outsource millions of jobs, Craig S. Smith reports encouraging news in the *New York Times* for those who believe we've been so busy working we've forgotten how to live. A French woman, Corinne Maier, wrote a book encouraging more sloth in the disinterested corporate workplace. And to whom would we look for a model of leisurely living but the French?—who already work less than people in other developed countries: nearly 300 fewer hours per year than Americans.

Maier's book, a tongue-in cheek slacker manifesto entitled, *Bonjour Paresse* (translated, *Hello Laziness,* a play on *Bonjour Tristesse*, Françoise Sagan's 1954 best seller that recounted a worldly woman's cynical approach to relationships and sex.), became an overnight best-seller in France. The book answers the question: "Can we work in a corporation and contest the system, or must we be blind and docile and adhere to everything that the corporation says?"

Maier became a countercultural heroine by encouraging French workers to adopt a strategy of "active disengagement" that eschews the Anglo-Saxon work ethic and openly embraces sloth. At a time when the IMF is encouraging European workers to work longer and harder, Maier argues that France's ossified corporate culture no longer offers rank-and-file employees prospects of success, so the best way to fight them is by spreading "gangrene from within" by loafing on the job. The book is aimed at "midlevel executives, white-collar workers, neo-slaves, the damned of the tertiary sector."

Typical of France's intelligentsia, she's overeducated and underemployed. Before earning a doctorate in psychoanalysis, she studied international relations and economics at the elite National Foundation of Political Sciences. She works 20 hours a week writing dry economic reports at the state electric utility, Électricité de France, for which she is paid about $2,000 a month. Many Americans whose jobs have been outsourced are also underemployed and overeducated for the kind of work they can find. With more workers than jobs, corporations aren't inclined to treat its workers well. Maier points out that French companies aren't meritocracies, any more than are American ones. Everything depends on where you went to school, what your connections are.

Her book, subtitled *The Art and Necessity of Doing the Least Possible in a Corporation*, has chapters titled "The Morons Who Are Sitting Next To You" and "Beautiful Swindles." She calls corporate culture "crystallization of the stupidity of a group of people at a given moment." Her solution: people who dislike what they do should "discreetly disengage." If done correctly—and she gives a few tips, such as looking busy by always carrying a stack of files—few co-workers will notice, and those who do will be too worried about rocking the boat to complain.

The book is a counterpoint to efforts by the center-right government to repair the damage done to French work habits by decades of Socialist rule, which enacted a 35-hour work week. What would we do without the indomitable Gallic *joie de vivre*?

August 18: * Carl Sagan said, "To make an apple pie from scratch, you must first invent the universe." To make a pie, you have to find your own way, which is the own way of the universe. Because of the interdependence of all beings, they will harmonize if left alone and not forced into conformity with some arbitrary, artificial notion of order. This harmony will emerge "tzu-jan," of itself, without external compulsion. This is the meaning of the Tao, so "they" say.

August 19: * The great Stoic Cicero describes, in his "Dream of Scipio Africanus the Younger," a supposed vision of the youth who lived c. 185-129 B.C., who saw his grandfather, Scipio Africanus the Elder (237-183 B.C.), who years before had invaded Africa and defeated Hannibal. In this dream, the Elder Africanus reveals to his grandson a new spiritual view of the universe and man's place in it. He points out how insignificant is the portion of land that belongs to the Romans in the larger scheme of things. He says, "The spirit is the true self, not bodily that form which can be pointed to by finger… [T]hat which is always in motion is eternal; but that which communicates motion to something else, but is itself moved by another force, necessarily ceases to live when this motion ends. Therefore, only that which moves itself never ceases its motion, because it never abandons itself; …it is the source and first cause of motion in all other things that are moved…[W]hatever moves of itself is eternal…[Whatever] possesses a spirit is moved by an inner impulse of its own; for that is the peculiar nature and property of a spirit. And as a spirit is the only force that moves of itself, it has no beginning and is immortal."

August 20: * Plutarch tells of Romulus, who with his twin Remus, were born of a virgin of Aeneas' royal line, who had been forced by her father Amulius, brother of King Numitor of Alba, to become a Vestal Virgin. When the boys were born, Amulius gave them to a servant to dispose of. The servant put them in a small boat and cast them into the river. (Sound familiar? The story of a child being cast into the river appears in lore around the world.) The boat eventually came aground under a fig tree, where a she-wolf found the babies and nursed them, while a woodpecker brought them food. When they grew up and had undergone some hardships and testings, the boys decided to establish a city where they had spent their infancy. But they had an argument and Romulus slew his brother, and then he proceeded to found his city, Rome. At the end of his life, Romulus simply disappeared. Later, Julius Proculus related to the forum how, as he was been traveling on the road, he had seen Romulus coming to meet him, "looking taller and comelier than ever." He was dressed in shining and flaming armor. When Proculus asked Romulus why he had deserted his people, Romulus replied, "It pleased the gods, O Proculus, that we, who came from them, should remain so long a time amongst men as we did; and having built a city to be the greatest in the world for empire and glory, should again return to heaven…"

August 21: * Google has been cursed by a new practice called "Google-bombing," wherein people conspire to have a particular phrase linked to a given Web page. If you type in "miserable failure," you will be linked to the White House Website and the official biography of President George W. Bush. If you type in "more evil than Satan himself," you will be linked to Microsoft's home page.

August 22: * More on the liminal, or threshold idea that applies as much to ourselves as to fish. Artist James Prosek talks about why he loves to paint trout as they jump out of the water: "I represent them when they hit our world, the moment when they break the surface of the water, that mysterious in-between place. The moment they come out of the water and hit the sunlight is the moment when they are most vibrant and they are very much still alive."

August 23: * Albert Einstein, describing how atoms can share information instantly, called the phenomenon "spooky action at a distance."

* There are more Irish in New York City than in Dublin, Ireland; more Italians in New York City than in Rome, Italy; and more Jews

in New York City than in Tel Aviv, Israel.

August 24: * Computer scientist Richard Shoup, president of the Boundary Institute in Saratoga, CA, after studying random pre- and post-9/11 data, said, "The data seem to show that observation can change things, that maybe thoughts affect the world." As long ago as my high school science classes, we knew that it was impossible to observe an electron's progress without changing its course. (I think because the light necessary to see it interfered with its natural course... but that was many, many years ago.) Wayne Dyer wrote a book called *The Power of Intention* that I have never read—I've never read anything by him. But I've seen a quote from that book to the effect that intention is not "something *you do*, but rather a force that exists in the universe as an invisible field of energy."

August 25: * Statisticians say that improbable occurrences like coincidences are more likely to happen than we think. Still, we're fascinated when strange coincidences pop up. We begin to wonder: Is there a deeper order, an overarching principle in the universe that moves us along? Are events in our lives objective or subjective? Many of the remarkable feats our brains regularly perform depend on our penchant for noticing coincidences and making meaningful connections. Once my friends Mike and Mary Frances Allen invited me over to view a training film from Mike's oil company. I learned there is something called the reticular activating system that filters out millions of bits of information that bombard us every day and allows through only what we need at the moment. Otherwise, we would be overwhelmed all the time and wouldn't be able to function. When something new comes up—say someone is diagnosed with a disease we never heard of, and we want to learn more—suddenly we begin to see that name everywhere we look. The information was there all along, but we filtered it out because we didn't need it. This may explain many things we take to be synchronistic events.

August 26: * On this date in 1920, the 19th Amendment to the U.S. Constitution, guaranteeing American women the right to vote, was declared in effect. My mother was seventeen years old.

* Chicago has the world's second largest Polish population.

August 27: * For centuries in Europe, formal marriage was a private contract between landed families, designed to insure that property remained within a particular lineage. Wealthy families married other families, forging political and social alliances. During the Reformation, the early Protestant idea of "companionate marriage" appeared, meaning that the emotional bond between husband and wife became an end in itself. This was a marked departure from the Catholic idea of chastity, which considered earthly marriage a more or less unfortunate necessity meant to accommodate human weakness. As Paul put it, "It is better to marry than to burn," although he sounds as if it's just the lesser of two evils.

At the time Luther nailed his proclamations to the door, Catholics had no requirements that a priest be present at a wedding. Vows taken in private were considered binding enough. After Luther's time, northern European Protestants required, for the first time, a public ceremony in the presence of witnesses. In England, a couple's intention to marry was proclaimed in church (banns) on three consecutive Sundays, giving the congregation time to determine if either party was committed elsewhere. State-issued marriage licenses were well-to-do families' alternative to the banns. Not until the confessional diaries and novels of the late 18th and 19th centuries began to influence bourgeois notions of "connubial felicity," to use Jane Austen's term, did romance become part of marriage.

Now, too many marriages end because one party is disillusioned by the lack of "romance," especially after several years. But other economically comfortable ones end because one partner insists on dictating to the other. Marriage becomes a *power struggle.* Living in even minimal bondage is stressful, and often crisis erupts at mid-life, when stress of the suppressed partner can no longer be contained.

August 28: * Conservative journalist Jonathan Rauch writes in his book *Gay Marriage,* which has an endorsement by George Will, that he believes legalizing gay marriage would impose social discipline upon the couples. "The gay rights era will be over and gay responsibility era will begin…no other institution [except marriage] has the power to turn narcissism into partnership, lust into devotion, strangers into kin." Just as society compels married heterosexuals to maintain a certain level of conduct, so gay couples would be expected to behave the same way. He believes giving gays rights would put an end to gay bath houses and the like.

August 29: * A false sense of security is often what does people in.

* Cardiac stents, which were designed to treat men, often won't fit in a woman's blood vessels. A few years ago, someone announced on the news that men had more brain cells than women, so they must be smarter. Not quite so. Men have *less* gray matter (the thinking part) than women, and *more* white matter (the spatial task part). Men have more neurons but fewer neural connections. Besides, men and women use different parts of their brains for the same task. It's like comparing apples and oranges.

August 30: * The World Economic Foundation, rating job opportunities, pay, political representation, health care and education, found (in 2005) that women in Sweden, Norway and Iceland had the highest standards (for women) in the world. The U.S. ranks 17th. China and India are 33rd. and 53rd, respectively. The worst off are the women of Egypt.

* For my birthday, here's John Mortimer: "The ageing process rushes up, pushes you over and runs off laughing. No one should grow old who isn't ready to appear ridiculous."

August 31: * Tolerance is better than extinction. Bill said this about one subject, but as I think about it, it applies to everything.

* The smallest sovereignty in the world is the Sovereign Military Order of Malta (SMOM), located inside Rome, Italy. It has an area of two tennis courts, and as of 2001, a population of 80, 20 less people than the Vatican, and like the Vatican is a sovereignty under international law.

* Damascus, Syria, was flourishing a couple of thousand years before Rome was founded in 753 BC, making it the oldest continuously inhabited city in existence.

* For the first time Inuit of the Canadian Northwest Territories are seeing robins, for which they have no name. Since the 1970s loss of sea ice equal to the size of Texas and Arizona combined has occurred north of the Arctic Circle.

September

September 1: * Every autumn monarch butterflies born east of the Rockies and from as far north as Canada, fly thousands of miles to Mexico. They are not guided by memory, for no one butterfly lives long enough to make the round trip. But each year millions find their way to the same fifty acres of forest in Mexico's Neovolcanic Mountains. Monarchs living west of the Rockies have a shorter migration: they head for the Pacific coast.

September 2: * On this date in 1945 Japan formally surrendered aboard the USS Missouri, ending WWII. My writer friend Bob Quinn was on a nearby ship and "witnessed" it from afar.

* Harriet Beecher Stowe: "In the gates of eternity the black or the white hold each other with an equal clasp."

September 3: * In 1964 a Swiss physicist named J. S. Bell proposed a theory that was confirmed in 1972 by another physicist, Alain Aspect, working at the University of Paris. It proved, in effect, that the world is inseparable. Everything is connected to everything else, and everything affects everything else. By 1975, this was being hailed as "the most profound discovery in the history of science" by physicists working at the University of California at Berkeley on a government-sponsored grant to prove for themselves that the theory is correct.

September 4: * The Dionysiac months began in September when the grapes and wheat were ripe and reached a climax in December when the Dionysiac festivals were held. The followers of Dionysus experienced religious frenzy, induced with the aid of wine, music and dancing at Dionysus' rites, which celebrated orgiastically the earth's fertility, as well as the idea of mortals achieving union with the god.

* One of the more disgraceful incidents in our country's history occurred on this date in 1957 when Arkansas governor Earl Faubus called out the National Guard to prevent nine black students from entering Central High School in Little Rock.

September 5: * It's hard to understand why someone would destroy his life with alcohol or drugs or gambling. But psychologist Marion Woodman says addicts can't trust reality. Their ability to rely on their own perceptions has been pulled out from under them, and there's an absence of trust at their core. They're constantly struggling to approximate or simulate reality, and they can't trust their own simulation either, because it keeps changing. What is ultimately real for them is the absence of reality. That's why they can lie with a straight face and expect people to believe them.

There's a physical change in the brains of addicts. They use the addiction to escape reality, and soon new neural pathways form that lead them back to the addiction whenever they're called on to cope with a difficult situation. When we *must* cope, pathways form in our brain that help us cope better at our next challenge. Over a lifetime, we develop good coping habits. That's what character is: the ability to do the right thing when called on. The addict, having avoided this responsibility, has actually destroyed his character.

* On this day in 1972, we didn't know it then, but the new era of terrorism had already begun when Palestinian guerrillas attacked the Israeli delegation at the Olympic Games in Munich. Eleven Israelis, five guerrillas, and a police officer were killed.

September 6: * As a child I read about "bundling" and didn't believe it really ever happened. But the tradition, like all primitive sex practices, was based on economic conditions. In the cold Scottish Highlands, and even in the cold American colonies, when a young man came to call on a young woman in her freezing house, the couple went to bed. For some, there was a "bundling board" that separated the two. In Scotland, the young woman's legs were inserted into one large stocking, which her mother tied above her knees. If the couple survived this routine and went on to marry, and the marriage didn't work out, they could go the Chapel of St. Coivan where, once a year all couples who were dissatisfied were blindfolded and were told to walk around the church. When St. Coivan called out "greimich" ("seize"), each man had to grab a woman. That woman was to be his wife for at least the next year.

Another tradition was called "handfasting." A couple could live together with or without their parents' permission for up to a year while they decided if they wanted to marry. If they did decide to marry, the wedding took place one day after the twelve months was up. If any children had been born in the meantime, the child became the responsibility of the man, and the woman's reputation was not sullied. This custom died out in the early sixteenth century.

In the Shetland Islands, even in the nineteenth century, on the day before the wedding, the best man slept with the bride-to-be.

September 7: * To recognize our own projections, to become aware of the unconscious dynamics by which we have lived, and to perceive new needs, does not mean having to demolish certain external situations, nor does it mean that this is the only possible solution. The real change is essentially an inner one, involving a new way of seeing things, and an emotional detachment that allows us to face reality without being crushed by it.

* In 1940 on this day, the Nazis began the initial blitz on London. British friends who were there said it was so bad that if anyone had told them how many times they would have to endure these bombings, they might have said, "I can't possibly take it." But they did.

* In 2002, Mswati II, 34-year-old son of King Sobhuza II, took over in Swaziland. Sobhuza had over 100 wives, but so far Mswati has only nine.

September 8: * Joseph Campbell says, "If you follow your bliss, you put yourself on a kind of track that has been there all the while, waiting for you, and the life you ought to be living is the one you are living. When you can see that, you begin to meet people who are in the field of your bliss, and they open doors to you. I say, follow your bliss, don't be afraid, and doors will open."

But if for some reason you feel your life's calling is in danger, suddenly a primal part of you may come into play. You become a force of nature, so strong that life could not be taken away from you. It's pure energy. In other words, the moment you definitely commit yourself, then Providence moves too.

There are two aspects of commitment to our life's calling. There is a commitment to take action. The second more subtle aspect to commitment is the *ground of being* for taking action. Our commitment shifts when the ground of being that allows us to take action in a way that furthers our overall quest, that allows synchronicity to occur, shifts, and vice versa. It is a different type of commitment, a different base for taking action. It's what theologian Martin Buber calls the "grand will" as opposed to the "puny, unfree will." Buber says most people believe in destiny, believe it stands in need of them. They know they must go out with their whole being. Matters won't turn out according to their decision. Buber says that after a person sacrifices his "unfree will" that is controlled by things and instincts, then he intervenes no more, "but at the same time he does not let things merely happen. He listens to what is emerging from himself, to the course of being in the world; not in order to be supported by it, but in order to bring it to reality as it desires."

The ground of being that enables this "grand will" to operate is that of physicist David Bohm's implicate order—being a part of the unfolding process of the universe. It manifests in living our life by doing, taking action now. We devote our life to doing what we need to do every day. We pay attention to all that is going on around us.

There is a paradox at work. Something important has shifted, and what has shifted fundamentally is the "I": one's sense of identity. We're now part of the unfolding, generative process, and in this state of being, we're no longer controlled by things and instincts.

Carl Jung: "I have a sense of destiny as though my life was assigned to me by fate and had to be fulfilled. This gave me an inner security."

September 9: * I find it peculiar that our culture is playing a sort of Russian roulette with ourselves and the earth. What causes this neurosis? How close can we come to the edge without going over?

Geologists tell us that the earth has remarkable resiliency to withstand assaults on the delicate balance necessary to maintain life. Earth will survive, but some of the species may not. The human race, maybe.

* This day in 1976, Mao Tse-tung finally died at the age of 82.

September 10: * W. B. Yeats gave Iseult Gonne some advice that she reminded him of more than once in letters: (1) To give value to things or people, make a sacrifice for them. (2) Only accept such thoughts and emotions as are seasonal. (3) Before the inevitable, bow and say, "Thy will be done." This may not have been exactly what Yeats said, but it is what Iseult got out of it.

Iseult was a thoughtful woman (the daughter of Yeats' lifelong love, Maud) who was 22 when she wrote to him: "I think the secret [of "the winning of Quiet"—Yeats' term—of the spirit] is this: make duty a game and game a duty, bring fancy into work and seriousness into play; then both play and work seem good for they hold each other company and are no longer lonely in their tasks. A green lawn planted with trees where the sun and shade are equally divided on the grass in a trembling watery intertwining, appears to me as the symbol of quiet…in the heart of the contrasts of life, the only quiet that is really quiet because it leaves nothing out."

September 11: * Maud Gonne makes the statement in her autobiography, *A Servant of the Queen*: "The only consolation I had ever found for sorrow was in redoubled work."

In another place in this same autobiography, describing the terrible famine in Ireland, she quotes St. Thomas, in *Summa Theologica Quest.* 66 Art. 2, on the rights of property when opposed to the right of life: "if…a need is so plain and pressing that clearly the urgent necessity has to be relieved…then the man may lawfully relieve his distress out of the property of another, taking it—either openly or secretly…."

She quotes His Holiness Pope Clement I: "The use of all things is to be common to all. It is an injustice to say this belongs to me, that to another. Hence the origin of contentions among men."

And His Holiness Pope Gregory the Great: "…the earth from which they sprang, and of which they are formed, belongs to all men in common and therefore the fruits which the earth brings forth must belong without distinction to all."

And Cardinal Manning: "In case of extreme need of food, all goods become common property."

September 12: * Our existence can't be linear. A life lived in an authentically human way requires continual choices among various directions and possibilities, meaning that we can make mistakes and lose our way. But there are lessons to be learned on every path.

Concretism occurs in every literal question we put to someone, in every thrust of hard-headed advice, every penetration about how to live and what to do. Veniece Standley, with whom I studied archetypal symbolism for six years, used to say, "Run from someone who has all the answers." Why? The person who has the all the answers thinks his way is the only way. This is mental rape, which is just a metaphor for moving into someone's personal space in a crude manner and telling them how to think, or what beliefs to accept. There is a lot of rape going on in fundamentalist religions.

Rape (in whatever meaning) is a horror because it is an archetypal transgression. It forcibly crosses between two unrelated structures of consciousness, whose distance is described in the language of opposites: old woman/ young boy, young girl/ old man, virgin/lecher, white/ black, native/ foreigner, soldier/ civilian, master/ slave, beauty/ beast, upper class/ lower class, barbarian/ bourgeois, monstrous impulse/ wounded innocence. But this transgression is also a *connection* between these opposites. "Rape" is *control* over someone else. It puts the body's drive toward soul into a concrete metaphor. It forcibly ends the division between behavior and fantasy.

In myth, when the god Pan rapes, his assaults are *compulsions*, not so much attacks to destroy another as they are a clutching need to *possess* the other. Any time a fundamentalist tells you what to believe, that's his need to possess you, body and soul. Deviation from his "norm" is unthinkable. You *can't* believe something different from him; he won't allow it. Thus, fundamentalism is a compulsion.

* But here's the intriguing thing: What stops compulsion? In myth, the key, is *music (!!)*, sound of the nymphs. Syrinx, Echo, and Pitys (who sighs—Nonnus—or moans when the wind blows through the pines) are the sounds of nature. The nymphs reflect nature to the ear. They teach listening, and *listening stops compulsion.* Nature, in other words, heals, if we stop to listen to it.

Is it any wonder that deposed Secretary of the Interior James Watt of Utah and Congresswoman Chenowith of Idaho both declared environmentalism is paganism? They would prefer to concrete over the rest of the earth and thus "purify" it of dirty, messy nature.

September 13: * It is believed that the coffee plant originated in Ethiopia, although the Arabians began cultivating it more than 1,400 years ago. At first it was used as food. The dried berries were mashed with fat and rolled into balls to be eaten. By the 1200s, Arabs had begun roasting the beans to make a drink—alcohol is forbidden by Islam. In the mid-1500s, coffee-drinking had spread to Turkey, and Turkish coffee is known around the world (but whoever hears of Arabian coffee?). From Turkey, coffee growing spread to Italy in the early 1600s, and it reached Brazil in the early 1700s. Today Brazil grows about one-fourth of the world's coffee. It was obvious very early that the bean was a stimulant, and for that reason, drinking coffee was outlawed in some countries. Anyone caught drinking it was beaten or, in some places, put to death.

September 14:* In 2004, the richest place in the world was New York. The second was Moscow. The richest man in the world was Bill Gates, with 46.6 billion dollars. Warren Buffett was second with 42.9 billion. There were 587 billionaires in the world, 64 more than in 2003. But in the US, the gap between the very wealthy and the poor widened, and more people slipped down out of the middle class. History has taught us that a nation cannot survive without a strong middle class. Nor can a democracy thrive without educated citizens. (Laura Bush is strong on that point.) India agrees.

Muhammad taught that educated men were next to angels and that "the scholar's ink is more sacred than the blood of martyrs." The Catholic clergy, on the other hand, once wanted the masses kept in the dark so they could be more easily manipulated. While Europe was still mired in ignorance during the Dark Ages, almost everone in ninth-century Baghdad could read and write. It was a city of book-sellers, libraries, bathhouses, gardens, and game parks. Harun al-Rashid was the first chess-playing caliph, and Baghdadis also played checkers and backgammon. Translators rendered Greek works into Arabic, where they were preserved for several centuries until they were translated into European languages.

Arts and sciences flourished in Baghdad: literature, music, calligraphy, philosophy, mathematics, chemistry, history.

Osama bin Laden recently said that Colin Powell (but did Powell deserve to be included? Weren't meetings held behind closed doors that Cheney suggested Powell not be invited to attend?) and Dick Cheney had destroyed Baghdad worse than Hulagu (a Mongol general who sacked the city in 1258). For more on Hulagu, Genghis

Khan and their wives, see my *Encyclopedia of Traditional Epics.* Since Baghdad was thought to be the center from which much of Western Civilization sprang, the destruction of its antiquities wipes out most of our own history. Will future generations look kindly on us for this?

September 15: * Jeffrey Goldberg, in a *New Yorker* article entitled "Among the Settlers: Will they destroy Israel?", says, "…the ideologues of the settlement movement have stripped their religion of all love but self-love; they have placed themselves at the center of God's drama on earth; and they interpret their holy scriptures to prove that their enemies are supernaturally evil and undeserving of even small mercies." He quotes Michael Tarazi, Harvard-trained legal advisor to the Palestinian negotiating team, who talks about dissolution of Israel as a haven for the Jews: "Zionism in practice is about taking the land and getting rid of the people.…[T]he national-religious Zionists are dragging Israel in the direction of theocratic fascism…We have to look at the way the South Africans did it. The world is increasingly intolerant of the Zionist idea.…We have to make this an argument about apartheid."

* In 1963 on this date, a Sunday, one of the darkest incidents in our history occurred. Four children were killed when a bomb went off during church services at a black Baptist church in Birmingham, Alabama.

September 16: * King Coleus, or Old Coel the Splendid, a king in Ayrshire in Scotland at the end of the Roman period, inspired the nursery rhyme, "Old King Cole."

* Today in 1974 was a compassionate day in our history: President Gerald Ford announced conditional amnesty for Vietnam dissenters and draft evaders. Those were difficult days for everyone. I remember being uncertain whether to put out our flag or not, because some people thought the flag stood for war, and the war was very unpopular.

September 17: * If we could learn how to dialogue with one another at a deep level, we could find ways to relate that would dissolve the perception of separateness. A relatively few people working together in this way could have a profound effect on society because, according to physicist David Bohm, their consciousness is already woven into all. Bohm speaks of the human capacity for collective intelligence, for generative conversation and resulting coordinated action.

* On this date in 1862 the Union repelled the Confederate invasion of Maryland in the Battle of Antietem, where 23,100 were killed, wounded or captured, making it the bloodiest day in U.S. military history. All four of my great-grandfathers and even one great-great-grandfather fought in the War Between the States, all in Confederate forces, so family lore about why this war was *really* fought—at least by the common men who had no slaves and no interest in them—is far different than the textbook account. But then, history is always written by the winners.

September 18: * "There is a current that is taking us somewhere, and there is a creative intelligence underlying it." – Nina Utne

* Groups of animals:

A cloud of grasshoppers
A sloth of bears
A business of ferrets
A troop of monkeys
A plague of locusts
A bloat of hippos
An army of caterpillars
A crash of rhinos
An ostentation of peacocks
A trip of goats
A knot of toads
A rafter of turkeys
A skulk of foxes
A string of ponies
A gaggle of geese
A murder of crows
A stand of flamingos

* Psychologist Marion Woodman says that what is happening with addicts is that "the soul is trying to lead them into the presence of the divine if only they can understand the symbolism inherent in the addictive substance or behavior." In other words, the alcoholic is trying to find God, whether he realizes it or not.

September 19: * Apuleius tells the story of Eros and Psyche, where Psyche, her love gone and help from the gods denied, throws herself into the river. But it refuses her. In that moment of panic, Pan appears with his reflective other side, Echo (our reflective nature), and saves her from suicide. Thus, Pan (representing our instincts) has two natures: he is both destroyer and preserver. When we *pan*ic, it may be the first movement of nature that will yield (if we can hear the *echo* of *reflection*) a new insight into nature.

When we *pan*ic, we usually do something self-destructive. When we drink to dull pain, to help us forget our inadequacies, it may seem, momentarily, that we succeed. But alcohol, which under certain circumstances is a preservative, is also a destroyer and actually only magnifies the pain and makes our short-comings grow. It is possible, that in the aftermath of a drunken spree, Echo may appear to remind us of our folly, and in that time of reflection, we may come to understand that addictive behavior only exacerbates whatever problem we're trying to escape.

September 20: * "Faith is a matter of resisting evil and serving justice" – Rev. William Sloan Coffin

* This date in 1973 was a proud day for women when tennis great Billy Jean King finally shut the arrogant mouth of Bobby Riggs in straight sets: 6 – 4, 6 – 3, 6 – 3. In this winner-take-all match held in the Astrodome, Billy Jean walked away with $100,000 and the appreciation of women everywhere for redeeming our honor.

September 21: * Dr. Walter Wink, professor of biblical interpretation, Auburn Theological Seminary, New York City, interpreting the passage from Matthew, *But if anyone strikes you on the right cheek, turn the other also*: "Most people probably think of a right hook here, but a right hook would hit the left cheek. A left hook would strike the right cheek, but in Jesus' day the left hand was reserved for unclean tasks. Even to gesture with the left hand in a Semite society would bring shame on the one doing so. The only conceivable blow would be the back of the right hand. This is not a blow to injure, but to humiliate. It was always a 'one down' blow by a "superior" to an 'inferior': husband to wife, parent to child, master to servant, Roman to Jew. By turning the other cheek, the inferior is saying, 'I refuse to be humiliated by you. I am a human being, a child of God. You can kill me, but my soul is out of your reach.' This reaction is light years from the passive acquiescence ascribed to Jesus all these centuries."

September 22: * From 1690 to about 1720, there was a little-known "country," the Republic of Libertalia. It was located on Saint Mary's Island in the Indian Ocean. The Republic of Libertalia was a self-governing island operating as a peaceful, democratic society. It was better known as the base of operations for pirates such as Captain Kidd, Henry Every, and others.

September 23: * Joseph Campbell, who spent a lifetime studying the world's great mythologies, didn't start out in that direction. In the 1920s, while at Columbia University, he was one of the fastest half-milers in the world. He toured the country with Jackson Scholz, who went on to race in the 1924 Paris Olympics. Scholz was later portrayed in the movie *Chariots of Fire* as the American racing the Scot and the English runners. Campbell would have joined them, but at the Olympic trials in Honolulu, he lost his very last race by a hair's breath. He was so devastated that he rarely spoke about his own athletic career again.

Campbell, who became a professor at Sarah Lawrence, exhorted his students to "follow your bliss." At age 50, Campbell found his own bliss as he walked Bombay's streets, "bebrooding a few ideas." He wrote two massive journals, close to 800 pages, during his year-long travels to India and Japan in 1954-1955. His travels coalesced for him the existence of a common substratum to all the world's myths, a bedrock monomyth that emanates out in different local inflections of a single story. He called his life's work Comparative Mythology, and he spent his long life understanding how myths speak to us in our own lives, and by what myths we are living today. The one time I heard him in person—and got to shake his hand—he told us we need new myths to live by because *we have tried to make our myths factual history* and thus have drained them of power.

September 24: * When it comes to the loss of American jobs overseas, should we blame the invisible hand of the free market or the back of the hand from politicians? A new study by the AFL-CIO provides plenty of evidence that American workers have been slapped by the policies of the Bush administration over again.

The report finds that we have lost 2.7 million manufacturing jobs and nearly 900,000 professional service and information sector jobs since President Bush took office in January 2001. Of these job losses, the Economic Policy Institute estimates that 935,000 manufacturing jobs were lost due to our rising trade deficit. And Goldman Sachs estimates that 400,000 to 600,000 professional service and information sector jobs were shipped overseas.

But the causes of these job losses are even more revealing. Among the causes cited in the AFL-CIO study are:

U.S. tax laws reward corporations for using cheap labor overseas to the tune of $7 billion each year. Not only has the Bush administration refused to eliminate these giveaways, it has proposed creating even more tax incentives for U.S. companies that ship work overseas.

The second Bush administration routinely waived Buy American laws for federal purchases and opposed expansion of such provisions for Defense Dept. purchases.

The Commerce Dept. actively sponsored "conferences and workshops that encourage American companies to put operations and jobs in China."

September 25: * In New York and California and no telling where else next, there's a performance artist named Bill Talen who dresses up in a clerical collar and calls himself Reverend Billy, and he, his choir (in gold satin robes), and a three–piece band invade a franchise store like Starbucks or Wal-Mart or Barnes & Noble or Home Depot with his crusade against consumerism. In the Times Square Disney Store alone, he has staged more than thirty "retail interventions."

He calls his group the **Church of Stop Shopping**. He performs "cash register exorcisms" or "credit card exorcisms" and exhorts customers not to patronize franchise stores that have run the local merchants out of business. "We're drowning in a sea of identical details!" he likes to preach, and he leads them in prayer to "the God that is not a product." Before he begins, a few choir members circulate with rolls of duct tape to cover any visible logos on the congregation's clothing. Customers usually take his activist "sermon" good naturedly—in fact, in May, 2004, the National Trust for Historic Preservation put the entire state of Vermont on its "endangered" list and laid the blame explicitly on Wal-Mart—but in California, Starbucks got a court order enjoining him from coming within 250 yards of any of the 1,481 Starbucks franchises in the state. In 2000 a memo was circulated to the Manhattan Starbucks stores answering the question, "What should I do if Reverend Billy is in my store?"

At the 1999-2000 Obie awards ceremony, he won a "special citation" for his Reverend Billy work. He realizes the novelty of his campaign will eventually fade, but right now, he calls himself "this month's flavor."

September 26: * Primatologist Jane Goodall has found that all the great apes in captivity, chimpanzees, bonobos, gorillas, and orangutans, have not only learned American Sign Language, but have taught other of their own kind. The great apes can use computers. Goodall says there is a chimp in Japan who has learned to solve complex problems. She can replicate a set of numbers on the computer after the screen goes dead. Goodall says, "Her mind is clearly working the same way as ours, but actually much faster."

Furthermore, whales and dolphins communicate over long distances by using high frequency noises, while elephants use very low frequencies to communicate over long distances. Goodall says that elephants establish long-term friendships and recognize those individuals years later. They also have "extraordinary empathy and compassion" and sometimes even bury their dead.

* Birds are more intelligent than we realize. A crow "adopted" the kids at Annabeth's bus stop and insisted on playing with them before school, diving at them, landing on them, and sometimes pecking their heads until the bus arrived. Then, when it was time for the bus to bring them home, the bird would reappear and wait to play with them again. To watch him would leave no doubt that the crow was playing. Parrots can learn a large number of words, can use them in the correct context, and can initiate conversations. One parrot that Goodall knows and can use 971 words.

Any owner of a horse, dog, or cat is aware of animal intelligence. Dogs and cats are much more perceptive than people, according to Goodall. My writer friend Ann Anderson would attest to that.

* Everyone who could get to a TV was watching on this night in 1960 for the Kennedy versus Nixon debate. Debating on camera was a new idea, and the camera was not kind to Nixon, who had a

five o'clock shadow. That appearance won the election for Kennedy.

September 27: * Neurobiologist Emily Brandon of U.of Rochester Medical Center says we have at least eight-and-a-half kinds of intelligence we should exercise (on the "use it or lose it" principle). Harvard prof Howard Gardner outlines brain exercises for eight in his book *Frames of Mind: The Theory of Multiple Intelligence.*

Naturalist Intelligence: the ability to recognize and categorize nature. To develop it: learn names of plants and birds in your garden, pay attention to season changes, watch nature programs.

Linguistic Intelligence: sensitivity to the meaning of words. To develop it: read a book and discuss it with a friend or book club, write a poem, keep a journal, do crossword puzzles.

Intrapersonal Intelligence: access to one's own feelings. To develop it: spend time in reflection, record and analyze your dreams.

Musical Intelligence: sensitivity to pitch, melody, rhythm, and the emotions sounds evoke. To develop it: attend musical performances, learn to read music, sing, make up your own song.

Interpersonal Intelligence: the ability to recognize the temperaments, motivations, and intentions of others. To develop it: people-watch, listen to people, read biographies and autobiographies.

Spatial Intelligence: the ability to perceive the world accurately and transform, modify, and re-create that perception. To develop it: sculpt in clay, draw or paint objects in front of you, read a map or draw a map, listen to oral map directions and try to picture the route, do jigsaw puzzles or mazes, play blocks with your child.

Bodily-Kinesthetic Intelligence: the ability to use the body in differentiated and skilled ways for both expressive and goal-directed purposes. To develop it: play a sport, learn a craft, dance, take up yoga, build a model.

Logical-Mathematical Intelligence: the ability to solve mathematical and logical problems through inductive and deductive reasoning. To develop it: play games that require logic, like dominoes or chess or cards, do logic puzzles or brain teasers, go to a science museum, learn to program your computer, use a telescope or microscope to get a new perspective on the world, balance your checkbook by hand before reaching for the calculator.

Spiritualist-Existential Intelligence: the proclivity to ponder questions about life, death, and ultimate realities. It wasn't part of Gardner's original group, but psychological researchers like Robert Emmons, PhD, claim that it fits Garnder's criteria as a full-fledged intelligence. To develop it: identify a theme in your life, analyze your feelings about life after death, think what your purpose is, learn about a different religion, think about your relationship with your pet and whether it understands you.

September 28: * In 2003 Fareed Zakaria, editor of *Newsweek International*, observed after speaking to government officials in dozens of countries around the world, that almost every country that had had dealings with the Bush Administration had felt humiliated by it. *Humiliated*. Wealthy people have to be very careful not to appear arrogant to others. That's what diplomats are for. At the moment America is not powerful because people like us. Our power is a product of dollars and guns. But historical epics invariably blame the downfall of the rich and powerful on *hubris*.

September 29: * While doing graduate study, I came across a book in the library containing a large black and white photograph that affected me deeply. I knew I couldn't just close the book on that image. I photocopied it, but I don't remember the name of the book. It might have been one edited by Jacob Drachler called *African Heritage* (London: Collier Macmillan, 1963 and 1975). The picture was at the beginning of a section entitled "The Rise of Racism." It shows a black man caught in something that looks like fishnet. He has manacles on his legs and hands. His expression is one of profound despair. The reason I remember the picture so well is that I have it before me now. I have never been able to get it out of my mind. How could one human being do that to another?

September 30: * The Amazon rainforest produces more than 20% the world's oxygen supply. The Amazon River pushes so much water into the Atlantic that, more than 100 miles at sea, off the mouth of the river, one can dip fresh water out of the ocean. The volume of water in the Amazon is greater than the next eight largest rivers in the world combined and three times the flow of all rivers in the US.

*Antarctica is the only land that is not owned by any country.

Ninety percent of the world's ice covers Antarctica. This ice also represents seventy percent of all the fresh water in the world. As strange as it sounds, however, Antarctica is essentially a desert. The average yearly total precipitation is about two inches. Although covered with ice (all but 0.4% of it), Antarctica is the driest place on the planet, with an absolute humidity lower than the Gobi desert.

* Americans wonder why much of the world hates us so. Ian Buruma and Avishai Margalit provide answers in *Occidentalism: The West in the Eyes of its Enemies* (Penguin, 2004). These are things we've heard our friend Omar Pound say. (Omar specialized in Arabic Studies and taught in Morocco at one time.) "Occidentalism" reaches back to Japan in 1930 and before. When Japan attacked Pearl Harbor, people all over the Orient rejoiced. The war against the West was a war against a poisonous materialist society built on Jewish financial capitalist power. Eastern culture was spiritual and profound, whereas ours was shallow, rootless, heartless, cruel. The East was holistic; the West, specialized. The East was spiritual; the West, scientific and industrialized. The philosopher Nishitani Keiji blamed the Reformation, the Renaissance, and the emergence of natural science for the destruction of a unified spiritual culture in Europe. The West also meant colonialism, and to some extent, it still does, through its multinational corporations and global capitalism. Now, excluding Japan, the East and the Middle East do not like our pop excesses, foreign policy, or sexual license.

Hitler said, "American civilization is of a purely mechanized nature. Without mechanization, America would disintegrate more swiftly than India....my feelings against Americanism are feelings of hatred and deep repugnance." His feelings were echoed in France.

Now we are looked upon as depraved. Our trading system is seen as ruthless. Our exposed women are regarded by devout Muslims and even ultra-orthodox Jews as whores. Even our European "friends" see us as arrogant and recalcitrant.

"Religious authority is already having a dangerous influence on political governance," the authors say. They warn against "the temptation to fight fire with fire." Omar Pound has told us the same thing. The East expects to be reasoned with as an equal.

October

October 1: * There is basic integrity in a stone that unmasks sham and demands honesty. It might be wise to keep a pet rock. If you want to know the truth of a matter, ask a stone. At times when I am so fake to others or even to myself that I hardly recognize the truth anymore, I can hold the smooth surface of a simple rock in my palm and try to tell the same untruth or half-truth. It can't be done. You can't be dishonest to a stone. If you don't believe me, try it.

October 2: * By listening to our body, "tuning in," we find our larger place in the universe. By connecting inside, we connect to the larger world. Carl Jung says, "The more a man lays stress on false possessions, and the less sensitivity he has for what is essential, the less satisfying is his life."

* On this date in 1967, Thurgood Marshall was sworn in as the first black person on the Supreme Court.

October 3: * In Hindu cosmology, the Indian gods each has an animal to ride. Vishnu has an eagle called Garuda; Shiva rides a bull called Nanda; Ganesh dances on the back of a mouse. Ganesh himself has an elephant's head, due to a misfortune of his childhood which his father Shiva cut off in a jealous rage, believing that his wife Parvati had been impregnated by another god. When he realized his error, Shiva vowed to bring his son back to life, by bestowing on him the head of the first person he saw. The first one happened to be an elephant.

Ganesh has a fat belly that you can rub if you want wealth and prosperity. With his powerful trunk, he can clear your path of obstacles. Many Hindus give statues of Ganesh a prominent place in the entryway of their home.

The elephant is a *mysterium tremendum*, a living mystery. D. H. Lawrence calls them oldest and wisest of beasts. Describing how they mate in secret, "hiding their fire," he says, "They do not snatch, they do not tear:/ their massive blood/ moves as the moon-tides, near, more near,/ till they touch in flood." Elephants show enormous sensitivity. As a family they protect and nurture the young of the herd. They grieve when one of their number is lost. If you have ever looked into the eyes of an elephant in captivity, you see despondency.

October 4: * Symbolic interpretation of dragon-slaying: Only after a man succeeds in his heroic quest can he relate easily to women. He no longer finds them threatening. Misogynists are the way they are simply because they can't admit feeling threatened by women.

* Mary Hewitt: "True delicacy, that most beautiful heart-leaf of humanity, exhibits itself most significantly in little things."

October 5: * A pervasive feeling of disconnection is one of modern culture's greatest casualties. A hundred years ago, we walked on dirt roads; we rode animals that sweated, grunted, whose flesh touched our flesh. We looked into the eyes of the animal and into our own soul. D. H. Lawrence, in *St. Mawr*, describes a horse: "...in his dark eye, that looked...like a world beyond our world, there was a dark vitality glowing, and within the fire, another sort of wisdom."

October 6: * About 550 million years ago, there was literally an explosion of life forms, referred to as the Cambrian Explosion, or biology's Big Bang.. All the major animal groups suddenly, dramatically formed. It was one of those "quantum leaps."

Why didn't these creatures appear very gradually in the fossil record? A young Oxford zoologist named Andrew Parker has posited the "Light Switch Theory" which says that it was the development of vision in primitive animals that caused the sudden boom. Precambrian creatures, being unable to see, couldn't distinguish between friend and foe, but with the evolution of the eye, the size, shape, color and behavior of animals was apparent for the first time. Existing creatures either adapted or died out.

October 7: * When suffering drives us to question ourselves, a first level of response can be found on the philosophical or religious plane, in already existing systems that offer quick and ready answers to our problems. These are therefore collective answers and can never completely satisfy the individual. If we stop at this point, we inevitably become dogmatic, obliged to defend rigorously the principles we adhere to, without realizing that our rigidity and unbending orthodoxy conceal doubts. But if we succeed in sustaining the tension of uncertainty and keep up the search for *personal* answers, they may become a new philosophy for us, one we don't have to convince ourselves to believe.

The summons to our journey of inner discovery is not a justification for narcissism. We are still obliged to fulfill our commitments to others, to meet our responsibilities.

When we start to be honest about our own life, we recover the worth of our own journey. Life takes on a new meaning and our prayer, in the words of Kazantzakis, "is the report of a soldier to his general: This is what I did today,...these are the obstacles I found, this [is] how I plan to fight tomorrow." When we reject collective expectations and seek our own path, then justice returns.

October 8: * October is a time to express ingenuity and talents, to reap the abundant harvest of previous efforts, to prepare for a time of celebration. Soon this season will be followed by one of rest, introspection, and reenergizing for a time of new growth. My poet friend Jo Ann Lewis called these "the brandied days of autumn."

* We all have our weaknesses where dogs are concerned. George Washington actually stopped a battle once to return a straying fox terrier to enemy troops.

October 9: * We create barriers between each other by our fragmentary thought. Physicist David Bohm says that when these barriers dissolve, there arises one mind, where we are all one unit, but each person also retains his or her own individual awareness. "That one mind will still exist even when they separate, and when they come together, it will be as if they hadn't separated. It's actually a single intelligence that works with people who are moving in relationship with one another. Cues that pass from one to the other are being picked up with the same awareness."

October 10: * Forgiveness is good for the health. It cleanses out thoughts of negativity and replaces them with thoughts of understanding. When we release past happenings, we come to the realization that it can no longer harm us or control our actions.

It is a natural tendency for humans to hate those upon whom

they depend, so tension and animosity grow. Men have special problems in this area. They may be torn between fear and rage and are emotionally dependent but resentful of the one they're dependent on. Like an alcoholic struggling to recover from his addiction, each must share his hidden fear and rage, not with his spouse, but with another man. It takes more courage for a man to speak his emotional truths to another man. Then the fear and rage melt away. Jung once observed that we don't solve our problems, we outgrow them.

Jung said, "I have frequently seen people become neurotic when they content themselves with inadequate or wrong answers to the questions of life….Such people are usually confined within too narrow a spiritual horizon. Their life has not sufficient content, sufficient meaning. If they are enabled to develop into more spacious personalities, the neurosis generally disappears."

October 11: * Carl Sagan's *Cosmos* series, shown on PBS in 1980, showed how "billions and billions" of stars formed, how, incredibly, we're all made from the same stuff as those stars, and how we embody the cosmos's ability to know itself.

* Hubris has no place in the life of a man of God. The most widely respected evangelist ever is Billy Graham, who always took a very modest salary (at one point when Jim Bakker was drawing over $400,000, Graham was drawing $18,000) and lived in the same small home he'd always occupied. He was summoned to the White House by every President since Truman, but he tried to avoid getting directly involved in politics. He continues to preach the Word of God, to counsel the broken in spirit and provide charity for the down-trodden. He lives the love and humility he preaches.

Compare that with the man who, in 1981, called the Constitution "a marvelous document for the self-government by the Christian people." When he became a candidate for President, he had to admit to an affair his wife had known nothing about. In 1983 he claimed that his prayers were responsible for diverting the course of Hurricane Gloria. He made similar claims about Hurricane Felix in 1995 and Hurricane Isabel in 2003. In 1991 he said the Episcopalian, Presbyterian, Methodist and other mainline churches had "the spirit of the Antichrist." Later that year he said Planned Parenthood taught kids bestiality and homosexuality.

This same evangelist claimed, in 1992, that the political Left's persecution of Christians was worse than the Nazi's treatment of the Jews. In 1993, he said that NOW insisted that all women become lesbians. In 2001, he said the 9/11 attacks were God's punishment for the USA's embrace of "pagans, abortionists, feminists, gays, lesbians, the ACLU and the People for the American Way."

On August 22, 2005, he called for the assassination of Hugo Chavez, the socialist President of Venezuela. "...if he thinks we're trying to assassinate him, I think we really ought to go ahead and do it. It's a whole lot cheaper than starting a war. And I don't think any oil shipments will stop..."

He announced a fund-raising drive for 9/11 victims, then, after an investigation, returned a huge sum that he had diverted for his own ministry fund. And yet, when Katrina hit, his organization was one of two (the other being the Red Cross) that FEMA endorsed for people to send contributions!

Along with the deposed head of FEMA, it's time for Pat Robertson to retire. His over $100 million estate ought to hold him.

October 12:* We are faced with two tasks in life. The first is to differentiate ourselves from the unconscious matrix, to form our individual psyche. This results in structuring a personality centered in the ego, able to act in the world in accordance with conscious directives. It involves a clear separation of the conscious and unconscious worlds, and hence also the risk of an excessive one-sidedness of consciousness, which may lose all ties with the wholeness of which we're a part. This differentiation of the ego is indispensable to the development of civilization, but it also means the loss of connection with the instincts. The person who is one-directional and thus so efficient, loses his psychological depth. The equation might be: the higher the degree of efficiency, the more does existence lack breadth and depth.

So the second task in life is the harmonization of the various parts of the personality. There seems to be no place in our culture for fantasy, which Jung calls "the clearest expression of the specific activity of the psyche." We stop too soon in relating to the rest of nature. Take the rock: does it have consciousness? Physicist David Bohm says it is an abstraction to talk of nonliving matter. "You cannot think of existence as local. Yourself is actually the whole of mankind... everything is enfolded into everything. The entire past is enfolded into us in a very subtle way." If we reach deeply into ourselves, we are reaching into the very essence of humankind. When we do this, we reach the generating depth of consciousness common to the whole of humankind and that has its whole enfolded in it.

October 13: * It is an anthropological fact that societies that do not polarize gender roles, do not assign men and women opposite and well-defined roles, on the basis of "pure" masculinity and femininity, are much less aggressive.

Even if we live in a polarizing society, the mind has powers that allow us to go beyond our normal or habitual way of being. And when people join together and go beyond their habitual way of being as a group, even more possibilities open up.

But there is a difficulty with only one person changing. People call that person a great saint or mystic or leader, who can see past differences into a wholeness. Most of us have a block and feel we could never be this way. We never face the possibility because it is too disturbing, too frightening.

October 14: * A crucial part of our life's journey is the struggle to overcome our accumulated baggage in order ultimately to operate in the flow of the unfolding generative order.

* George Bernard Shaw said, "This is the true joy in life, the being used for a purpose recognized by yourself as a might one...the being a force of nature instead of a feverish, selfish little clod of ailments and grievances complaining that the world will not devote itself to making you happy."

October 15: * Maybe I was put here to learn patience. When I'm patient, there will be no need to soothe hurt feelings tomorrow because of some thoughtless thing I said or did today. By being patient with others, I'm investing in their success. I'm sending them a silent message: you can do it! This is a gift. Probably the greatest gift we could give to someone.

October 16: * Facts that ought to be in the *Texas Almanac*:

Distance from Beaumont to El Paso: 742 miles. Distance from Beaumont to Chicago: 770 miles

The world's first rodeo was in Pecos... July 4, 1883.

Gaslveston's Flagship Hotel is the only hotel in North America built over water.

The Heisman Trophy was named after John William Heisman who was the first full time coach for Rice University, Houston.

Brazoria County has more species of birds than any other area in North America.

Aransas Wildlife Refuge is the winter home of North America's only remaining flock of whooping cranes.

Jalapeno jelly originated in Lake Jackson in 1978.

The worst natural disaster in US history was the hurricane in Galveston in 1900 in which over 8000 lives were lost.

The first word spoken from the moon, July 20, 1969, was "Houston."

El Paso is closer to California than to Dallas.

King Ranch is larger than Rhode Island.

Tropical Storm Claudette brought a US rainfall record of 43" in 24 hours in and around Alvin in July 1979.

Texas is the only state to enter the US by TREATY, instead of by annexation. (This allows the Texas flag to fly at the same height as the US flag.)

A Live Oak tree near Fulton is estimated to be 1500 years old.

Caddo Lake is the only natural lake in the state.

Dr Pepper was invented in Waco in 1885. There is no period after Dr in Dr Pepper.

Texas has had six capital cities:

1. Washington-on-the-Brazos
2. Harrisburg
3. Galveston
4. Velasco
5. West Columbia
6. Austin

Austin's Capitol Dome is the only dome in the U.S. taller than the Capitol Building in Washington D.C. (by 7 feet).

The name Texas comes from the Hasini Indian word "tejas" meaning friends. Tejas is not Spanish for Texas.

The State animal is the armadillo. The armadillo always has four babies! She has one egg which splits into four and she either has four males or four females.

The first domed stadium in the US was the Houston Astrodome.

October 17: * According to Maud Gonne, during Queen Victoria's reign, 1,225,000 people died of famine in Ireland; 4,186,000 emigrated; 3,663,000 were evicted by the British from houses they or their fathers had built.

* This was sent to me as a true story:

One day, a poor Scottish farmer named Fleming, while trying to make a living for his family, heard a cry for help coming from a nearby bog. He dropped his tools and ran to the bog.

There, mired to his waist in black muck, was a terrified boy, screaming and struggling to free himself. Farmer Fleming saved the lad from what could have been a slow and terrifying death.

The next day, a fancy carriage pulled up to the Scotsman's sparse surroundings. An elegantly dressed nobleman stepped out and introduced himself as the father of the boy Farmer Fleming had saved.

"I want to repay you for saving my son's life," he said.

"No, I can't accept payment for what I did," the Scottish farmer replied waving off the offer.

At that moment, the farmer's own son came to the door of the family hovel, and the nobleman asked, "Is that your son?"

The farmer admitted proudly that the boy was indeed his son.

The nobleman said, "I'll make you a deal. Let me provide him with the level of education my own son will enjoy. If the lad is anything like his father, he'll no doubt grow to be a man we both will be proud of." And that he did.

Farmer Fleming's son attended the very best schools and in time, graduated from St. Mary's Hospital Medical School in London, and went on to become known throughout the world as the noted Sir Alexander Fleming, the discoverer of Penicillin.

Years afterward, the same nobleman's son who was saved from the bog was stricken with pneumonia.

What saved his life this time? Penicillin.

The name of the nobleman? Lord Randolph Churchill. His son's name? Sir Winston Churchill.

October 18: * I wish I understood more about Freemasonry. I've been around Masons all my life, but I have never understood why they were formed and what purpose they serve. I had a pen pal for many years, Horace A. Littlejohn, the father of one of my friends. Mr. Littlejohn, whose formal education stopped when he was in the fourth grade, was one of the wisest, widest-read people I have ever known, which is why I began writing him in the first place: I wanted some of that wisdom. When he died, he had a Masonic funeral, the first I had ever witnessed. Since Mr. Littlejohn knew a lot about the major philosophies of the world, I wonder what Freemasonry had to offer him.

Edward VII was Grand Master of English Freemasonry, which belongs to the "Scotch Rite," professes a belief in the "Great Architect" and is "a subterranean enemy of the Catholic Church," Maud Gonne says. French Freemasonry belongs to the rite of the "Grand Orient" which directs its war against religion in general, according to Maud Gonne.

October 19: * In 1643, Roger Williams, a clergyman and founder of Rhode Island, who had been banished from the Puritan Colonies for challenging theocratic authorities, wrote that there should be a "Wall of separation between the garden of the Church and the wilderness of the world" (meaning the predations of sectarian political leaders). In 1802 Thomas Jefferson borrowed those words, saying there should be a "wall of separation" between church and state. The difference between these two statements is that, while Williams felt it was necessary to protect the church from the state, Jefferson considered the greater need was to protect the state from the church.

October 20: * In France, performing arts workers can receive a small unemployment benefit if they work as much as three months per year. Although the sums are very modest, they are generous by American standards, where arts workers seldom receive anything. But the French payments provide a safety net for some hundred thousand artist and technicians in film, theater, dance, and the circus, allowing them to work when they can, to accept artistically challenging engagements that are poorly paid, to work in schools, and to bring the arts to poor areas. Why the United States is so reticent about financing the arts and yet NYSE chairman Richard Grasso's retirement package was in excess of $187,000,000 shows us where our priorities are in the U.S.

October 21: * Dr. James Hollis, who directs the Jung Center in Houston, said in a *Chronicle* interview: "One of the most dangerous things in the world is moral certainty." He says people who are opposed to rights for gay people may have fears about their own sexuality. Moral certainty is a defense against doubt and ambiguity. "But those things (doubt and ambiguity) are reasonable responses to the complexity of life. The attitude of 'if I'm right, then you're wrong' is the way fundamentalists of whatever ilk the world over see things." It is this attitude that put us at odds of our former allies.

October 22: * Congress got a 3.1% pay raise in 2003 and in 2004 while retirees on Social Security received only 1.4%, and, with so much outsourcing to India, Mexico and the Far East, many private workers were happy just to keep their jobs. Due to tough economic times, Congressional members could vote to forego their raises, but when the subject comes up, it is voted down. Over the last four years, their raises have totaled $18,000, which is more than the average married couple gets per year on Social Security.

* Within my lifetime, physicians and psychiatrists dismissed depression in women as "housewife's syndrome." They began to see hysteria everywhere until they were diagnosing every independent act by a woman, especially a women's rights action, as "hysterical" or just "nerves." In the not too distanct past, doctors recommended suffocating hysterical women until their fits stopped. They recommended beating them across the face with wet towels and embarrassing them in front of family and friends as a way of treating their "hysteria." The general belief was that higher education for women caused the uterus to atrophy.

October 23: * Baccus Cemetery sits in the midst of Ross Perot's Legacy Office Park in Plano, Collin County, now just an extension of North Dallas. The cemetery is part of a farm homestead built in 1845 by Lt. Henry Cook (1775-1865), who moved from Illinois to what was then known as Peters Colony. Hard on his heels, early the next year, 1846, my great-great-grandfather, William C. Miller, arrived with his family from Greene County, Illinois, also to settle in Peters Colony. Historical landmark status protects the cemetery from encroachment by more business. When you enter the front gate, the first monuments you come to mark the graves of my great-great grandparents, William Calop (Caleb?) Miller (Oct. 26, 1814 – May 25, 1898) and Hester (Esther) Ann King Miller (May 10, 1822 – July 15, 1902), and my great-grandparents, James Henry Miller (September 16, 1845 – February 11, 1922) and Martha Adeline Miller (August 31, 1846 – October 21, 1924). Beside them lies a sister of James Henry Miller, Nancy Jane Miller (November 1847 – April 3, 1905), and beside them, my grandfather's brother, Great-Uncle Samuel Lee Miller (April 17, 1877 – 1960) and his wife, Margaret Julietta Branaman Miller (July 6, 1890 – 1977). Great-Aunt Julietta referred to Baccus Cemetery (in letters to me) as being in "Frankford, Texas," which must be what that little area of Plano used to be called.

October 24: * Joseph Campbell's lifelong research into the world's mythology led him to the conclusion that the world's stories were based on an *even older common myth*. He says, "A rich environment of mythic lore was diffused with the neolithic arts of agriculture and settled village life across the whole face of the earth, from which elements have been drawn everywhere for the fashioning of hero myths, whether in Mexico of Quetzalcoatl, in Egypt of Osiris, in India of Krishna and the Buddha, in the Near East of Abraham or of Christ. Although I had the pleasure of meeting Campbell and hearing him speak in the early eighties, at the time I hadn't waded all the way through his immense oeuvre, and I hadn't yet done my own research for the epics books that I wrote a decade later. So I had to discover for myself the startling similarities between stories all over the world. According to researchers with access to original documents, often these myths would be based on a real person, who through many hundreds of years of story-telling, got transformed into a supernatural being. As Campbell says, "Zoroaster, the Buddha, and Christ seem to have been historical characters. Some of the others may not have been."

The biography of Gautama was turned into a supernatural life through a long process of accretion, for the function of myth-building is to interpret the *sense*, not to chronicle the *facts*, of a life. Campbell says that through such a process history is lost, but history also is made. Prof. Charles Guignebert, an expert on ancient texts at the Sorbonne, says that in the course of development of the Christian message, “Jesus the Nazarene disappeared and gave place to the glorified Christ.”

October 25: * The mother/nurturer/protector is our introduction to the nurturing principle of the earth itself. When we grow from our mother in order to establish our own identity, we sometimes sever the ties with qualities that are necessary for our survival as individuals and as a species. Sometimes in dreams a black Madonna will manifest herself, perhaps having to do with the consciousness in matter. She is an earth figure, the opposite of the frenzy, annihilation, ambition, competition and materialism that engulf us. We need to connect with this archetype because there must be a counterbalance to the power that drives us, ravaging the earth, that has to be transformed.

The conscious feminine nature involves an awareness of the energy of the rock, the love in the bird, the tree, the ocean—an awareness of the harmony of all things, an awareness of abiding within the world soul. We must reconnect with the harmony of the whole universe in the marrow of our bones.

October 26: * A bridge carries a roadway over what otherwise might be an impassable obstacle. On life’s roadway, the unconscious, childish side of the personality is just such an obstacle that can bring the ego down. It *will* bring the ego down unless it is recognized and honored. Images, in the form of prayer or a dream, or conjured from conscious imagination, are the bridges between the conscious and the unconscious, or archetypal, level where the child lives. Without that bridge, without a direct line, people sooner or later become depressed. The creative matrix is gone, and creativity dries up without that daily communication.

But.

The child knows all about magic. Its use is a manipulation of intuitive knowledge of things beyond cause and effect. The child has faith and belief. Because the child’s words are charged with the energy of belief, they have the power to create the child's reality.

When we affirm words of renewal about ourselves *that we believe*, and when we can *imagine* the results the way a child can, we release a positive response in every cell of the body.

Sometimes the impasse is a gap between people. But we're free to construct a bridge to cross the miles separating us physically or ideologically, which is just as divisive, maybe more so. In the instant that we're able to imagine bridging the gap, we are united in love with those from whom we'd felt distanced.

October 27: * I heard on television that Japanese believe the soul is located behind the navel. That makes sense, because where the baby is connected to her mother must be the first place where the baby received identity.

* Between Dec., 1811, and April, 1812, the most powerful series of quakes ever to hit the US rocked a million and a half square miles of the Mississippi River Valley. The river actually ran backwards, and the quakes changed the course of the War of 1812, In the midst of the devastation, quakes uncovered evidence of a shocking cold-blooded murder of a slave by two of Thomas Jefferson's nephews.

October 28: * In the Koran, the Power of Evil, or Satan, is called Iblis. Both are counterparts of the Zoroastrian Angra Mainyu. (Zoroastrianism has a much greater influence on our current traditions than we realize.) In later verses of the Koran, Iblis is described as a jinni: "and he broke the command of his Lord." This is much like the concept that Satan was a fallen angel.

Jinn (from whence "genie" comes, as well as "genius") are the old desert demons of pre-Mohammedan Arabs, taken over by Islam, whereas angels are from the Zoroastrian-biblical heritage. There are two kinds of jinn: those who have accepted Islam, and those who have not.

From the Koran: "God created man, like pottery, from sounding clay, and he created jinn from fire free from smoke."

October 29: * The word *Yahweh* is not of Hebrew origin but Arabic. Joseph Campbell says, "Hence we are forced…to agree with Mohammed's startling claim that people of his own Semitic stock were the first worshipers of the God proclaimed in the Bible." As a god of Semitic desert people, Allah reveals, like Yahweh, the features of a typical Semitic tribal deity, particularly that he is not immanent in nature but is separate, transcendent. Also, for each Semitic tribe the chief god is the protector and lawgiver of the local group only. He is made known in the local laws and customs.

Among the Aryans, whose chief gods were nature gods, there was a tendency to recognize the counterpart of one's own deities in the gods of alien cults. The tendency of Semites, Campbell says, "has always been toward exclusivism, separatism, and intolerance."

October 30: * Until after the death of Byzantine emperor Theodosius II in July of 450 and the invasion of Rome by Attila the Hun in 451, the church in Rome, the see of Peter, had played almost no role in the church councils which met to decide the official church belief about such things as the divinity of Jesus and the virgin birth. The meetings were held in places like Alexandria or Constantinople or nearby Chalcedo and were attended by hundreds of bishops of the Orient but scarcely a half-dozen from the West.

October 31: * This is the last day of the year on the old Celtic calendar. For the ancient Gaelic festival of Samhuinn, or Samhain (now Hallowe'en), special cakes were baked to ward off evil spirits and superstitions and to welcome good fortune. The Hallowe'en cake was always prepared with charms; if you found a button, you would have a singular pleasure of your own choosing; a horseshoe meant good luck, and a ring meant that you would soon marry.

The discovery of a coin in a dish of cream and oatmeal meant marriage.

These traditions carried over to today and also include charms and coins in Christmas puddings.

November

November 1: * The fire festival of Samhuinn (Samhain in Ireland) falls on October 31 and November 1, with celebrations taking place the previous evening. In Celtic times, on Samhuinn itself, ancestor worship and left-to-right sun-worship rituals were observed. The Otherworld became visible and was seen to be a happy place, but those who were tempted to enter it would be returned instantly, grow old immediately and die. Apples were exchanged as gifts bestowing eternal youth (hence the custom of "bobbing for apples").

The Celts were a mobile society. No one owned the land; it was held in trust by the nobles for the common good.

In many other cultures, the Day of the Dead is celebrated at the first of November. As far back as the ancient Celts, rituals honoring the return of the dead have been celebrated. In Mexico, a shrine is built in each home with pictures of departed ancestors and displays of their favorite objects and favorite foods, to make the returning ones feel welcome, appreciated and honored.

Early Christians took the Celtic rituals and, instead of animals being offered to Baal or the Assyrian-Babylonian gods En-lil and Marduk, they were offered to St. Martin. (See November 11.)

Today I remember Mother and Daddy and my grandparents, aunts and uncles, and their parents and their grandparents: a great parade of good people who lived good, honorable lives. Who can feel unworthy with such a heritage?

I also remember with great tenderness the pets who have served us so faithfully. It isn't right to describe animals as our inferiors, for they bring us gifts, even if we only half-way notice them. Animals link us to the mythic realm. They are messengers of the gods; they are gates through which we shift our consciousness.

When undomesticated animals are thrust into the human environment, they may suffer the same soul-loss so common among humans. More often, the animal brings us vitality. Whitman's "Song of Myself," talks of animals being placid and self-contained. They aren't "demented with the mania of owning things."

November 2: * I like the saying, "The evening of life comes bearing its own lamp." In the evening of life, there is time to contemplate the many misplacements of our faith along the way. To place faith in youth or physical beauty is to be disappointed all too soon, for nothing can prolong either. To place faith in wealth or fame is to realize, at length, that neither brings happiness. In the winter of our existence, we come face to face with the one reality: we must place our trust in Love because we have no other choice. Just to admit of the possibility of the existence of God brings a calm peace, a serene joy that seeps into every crevice of the soul. Then, yes, even at this late stage, magic is still possible.

November 3: * The breakdown of the immune system in the microcosm, the human body, is mirroring what is happening in the macrocosm, the earth. The immune system is breaking down. It can't help its trees; it can't help its biosphere. Can we let this happen to this earth that loves and cares for us?

Love is our constant.

November 4: * Neil Russack, who is Jewish, describes his aunts as urging him when he was a boy: "Eat, eat....What do the *goyim* (gentiles) know about life? They don't even know how to eat. Who knows when the pogroms will begin again; we will have to move; remember, keep everything liquid."

* Work is such an honorable word. "Work is love made visible." And Proverbs 16:3 says, "Commit your work to the Lord, and your plans will be established."

November 5: * Physicist David Bohm says we have to give a lot of attention to consciousness: "Consciousness itself requires very alert attention or else it will simply destroy itself. It's a very delicate mechanism. We have to think with everything we have...We have to think, as Einstein said, with feelings in our muscles...." He says that an essential feature of modern physics is that all things are in sympathy. Mach's principle is: "The whole is as necessary to the understanding of its parts, as the parts are necessary to the understanding of the whole." A Chinese proverb illustrates how the universe as a whole influences local events, and vice versa: "If you cut a blade of grass, you shake the universe."

November 6: * In the sub-tropical part of the United States, where we live, fall comes late. By mid to late November, many years, nighttime temperatures have finally dipped, at least a time or two, into the thirties. One of the first changes we see is the bald cypress trees, which gradually blush to a gentle orange. When I taught at the University of Houston, as I walked across the campus, I would marvel at the glorious cypress trees, and once I picked up some of the cypress balls that lay thick around one tree. I took these home and planted them and now have a couple of fine bald cypresses to remind me of my days on the U of H campus.

November 7: * In Islam the spiritual character of women is rated very low. At least one Shi'a text says they were created from the sediment of the sins of demons, to serve as temptations to sinners (men, of course). They aren't admitted to initiations, and are of value only as vehicles for entry into the world of spirits condemned temporarily to take on flesh in punishment for their sin—women themselves being without souls. Yet, in Shi'a mythology, Fatima, Mohammed's daughter, is a divine being, higher than even her father. Fatima married Mohammed's cousin Ali, who became Mohammed's successor. In fact, she is called the "Mother of her Father."

November 8: * At some time we have all experienced the phenomenon described by Hannah Arendt, who wrote in *The Life of the Mind* of "a timeless region, an eternal presence in complete quiet, lying beyond human clocks and calendars altogether ... the quiet of the Now in the time-pressed, time-tossed existence of man. ... This small non-time space in the very heart of time..."

* Fyodor Dostoyevsky, describing certain seizures, during which the epileptic experiences a sense of the metaphysical and a different awareness of time, wrote: "There are moments, and it is only a matter of a few seconds, when you feel the presence of the eternal harmony. ... A terrible thing is the frightful clearness with which it manifests itself and the rapture with which it fills you.... During these five seconds I live a whole human existence, and for that I would give my whole life and not think that I was paying too dearly."

Neurologist Oliver Sachs, said in *The New Yorker* that at times, as we're falling asleep, we may experience an involuntary jerk—a myoclonic jerk,. reflexes generated by primitive parts of the brain stem that have no intrinsic meaning. But they may be given meaning by being associated with an instantly improvised dream, such as falling over a cliff, which may be so vivid and may even have several "scenes." To the dreamer, they appear to start *before* the jerk, and yet apparently the entire dream mechanism has been stimulated by the first preconscious preception of the jerk. All of this elaborate restructuring of time in our mind occurs in a second or less.

November 9: * On this day in 1989 something momentous happened in Dechmont Forest, West Lothian, Scotland, and less than three years later, Scotland became the only country in the world to have commemorated an encounter with a UFO.

It happened this way: Bob Taylor, a forester employed by the Livingston Development Corporation was in the forest and came to a clearing he knew well. There he found a 25-foot-high round "something" with a rim around its middle. Then it changed color and became almost transparent. Two spherical figures with many outstretched limbs rolled out of the sphere and grabbed him by the trouser legs. Before Taylor fainted, he smelled a burning odor. Much later, when he recovered to find his trousers singed but no sphere, he brought the local police to the spot. They found giant twin tracks and about 30 holes in the ground, all angled outward. They looked as if they might have been legs of a giant pod. Spooky, huh?

The evidence was so strong that the Livingston Development Corporation, in January of 1992, placed a commemorative plaque—not on that spot, but by mistake, on a rock on Dechmont Law.

November 10: * Who says the brain/mind is all in the head? Like everything else, we are holistic. Take the immune system, which can be compared only to the brain in its degree of subtlety. The way it recognizes the pattern of an invading virus or foreign organism bears a striking resemblance to recognition properties of the brain. At the cell level, lymphocytes employ similar mechanism to those of nerve cells and may even contain receptor sites for brain transmitter molecules. The immune system therefore acts as a pattern recognition system which communicates information across the body and stores it as memory. During invasions by viruses the immune system may even be able to communicate in some direct way with the nervous system and hence with the brain itself. The immune system could therefore be said to depend on *meaning* for its activities. If the *meaning* of the body is taken to be its intelligent, coordinated activity in health, then disease is a degeneration or breakdown in *meaning*.

Is it possible that patterns, being formative fields of information, have an active role within the processes of matter, thought, and behavior? These fields of active, formative information are not simply fields of habitual response, but are closer to some form of *intelligence* that wells up from an underlying creative source. Synchronicity, or the *meaningful* coordination of events, may be a more appropriate description than causality alone.

November 11: * Besides being Veteran's Day in the United States, November 11 is a traditional Scottish quarter day, Martinmas (St. Martin's Mass—see November 1), on which you can get "Martin drunk," meaning *very* drunk, because St. Martin of Tours (c. 316-397) was the patron saint of reformed alcoholics. This is also the approximate date when the martin, of the swallow family, migrates to Britain....Maybe the martin was so-named because of the date of its appearance.

* Ill wind department: Our experiences with the natural disasters of Hurricanes Katrina and Rita help prepare us as a nation for terrorist threats or other acts of nature, like earthquakes. We have learned what is involved with moving large masses of humanity out of harm's way. We should all be better prepared. The government can't think of everything.

November 12: * At Egyptian royal funeral processions, there were dwarfs turning somersaults. In tombs, there are paintings of dwarfs (probably bushman prisoners) turning somersaults. That was to help the resurrection of the king, the idea being that resurrection is a kind of somersault. In a mother's womb, the baby often turns a somersault so that it comes out head first. So the somersault can denote the birth process, and this may be where the Egyptians got the idea.

November 13: * In a man, the positive *anima* (his feminine side) is the magic of life. The man who is not in contact with his *anima* is dry, dull, intellectual and rather lifeless. The *anima* is the stimulus to life. Everything that stimulates a man or fascinates him comes from the positive *anima*. If a man has a negative relationship to his *anima*, he becomes depressed, finds no pleasure in anything, and criticizes everything. If he is out of touch with his *anima*, he projects it onto women and always expects them to produce the stimulus and magic of life, because he can't do it himself. There are men who can only be happy if a warm, friendly, beautiful woman looks after them. In order to humanize their *anima*, they must not expect the magic of life from their partner.

November 14: * Something new must not be peacefully inserted into the old habits. There are certain new things that one must have the honesty to call new and to stand up for, because otherwise the new energy is lost. Jung said, "If one does not constantly walk forward, the past sucks one back. The past is like an enormous sucking wind that sucks one back all the time. If you don't go forward you regress....As soon as you begin to look backward sadly, even scornfully, it has you again."

People regress. Children return to the old home to visit, and they experience regressions of their feelings, their attitudes. The past catches them and many don't have the stamina to make a break. The old order knows in some unconscious way what it lacks, and when it comes into view, the old order wants to take it over and claim it for its own, even though a generation has come between. One has to leave the past to itself. "Let the dead bury their dead."

November 15: * While random events may always throw out patterns by pure chance, the essence of a synchronicity is that the particular pattern has a meaning or value for the individual who experiences it. Synchronicities act as mirrors to the inner processes of mind and take the forms of outer manifestations of interior transformations.

It is the nature of synchronicity to have meaning and to be associated with a progound activation of energy deep within the psyche. It is as if the formation of patterns within the unconscious mind is accompanied by physical patterns in the outer world. As psychic patterns are on the point of reaching consciousness then synchronicities reach their peak; they generally disappear as the individual becomes consciously aware of a new alignment of forces within his/her personality.

Synchronicities are therefore often associated with periods of transformation. It is as if this internal restructuring produces external resonances, or as if a burst of "mental energy" is propagated outward into the physical world.

November 16: * Here's a spooky story: In 1994, when Pulitzer Prize author Jeffrey Eugenides was writing *Middlesex,* he was trying to draw on the images of his grandparents in a photograph he'd seen only once ten years before. At that moment, he received in the mail the exact same photograph: His mother had had it restored.

In 1995, as he was trying to write about the burning of Smyrna in 1922 while at an artists' colony in the woods, he wandered into the mansion connected to the colony. As he passed the reading table, he noticed a book left by a former guest. It was a historical account called *Smyrna, 1922*: just what he needed.

One of the characters in his book had a condition he had once read about in a 1975 edition of the *New England Journal of Medicine*, although he hadn't read anything about it since. In 1996, Eugenides went with his wife who had to see her endocrinologist and he mentioned his need. The doctor reached around and brought forth the identical article—of which he had been the co-author.

He borrowed the nickname, Obscure Object, from a girl he had known in college and gave it to his love interest in the book. On the day he finished his novel, he went to dinner at the American Academy in Berlin—and there was the original Obscure Object!

November 17: * An old Chinese saying is that the one who speaks the right word will be heard a thousand miles away.

* The horn of plenty has been associated with Thanksgiving for decades. The symbol originated with the fertility goat-god Pan, or Baphomet. When the Greek god Zeus was a baby, he was suckled by a goat whose horn broke off and suddenly overflowed with fruit.

November 18: * All mythology is the playing out of some variant of two great mythologems. The mythology of the Great Mother is the great circle, the death-rebirth motif, the Eternal Return. They mythology of the Sky Father is the quest, the journey from innocence to experience, from dark to light, from home to the future. Each mythic cycle must be served. The halo associated with Christ is a relic of the solar aura of the Sky Father. The serpent associated with the maternal deities is spurned by the emergent patriarchy in Genesis.

November 19:* Scots have traditionally believed that if they die when they are abroad, their souls return to the land of their birth through underground passages, with caves as resting places along the way. This is the "low road" mentioned in "The Bonnie Banks o' Loch Lomon." The song may have originally been a conversation between two prisoners, one about to be executed and the other soon to be freed to return home by the usual, or "high road."

* I read this online: God may have created man before woman, but there's always a rough draft before the masterpiece.

November 20: * There are only three countries that are not on the metric system: Burma, Liberia (which was colonized by freed slaves from the USA, and the United States. In the 20th century, in the light of the new global economy, we began to move toward converting to the metric system. The U.S. Metric Board was assigned the task of helping to gradually integrate metrics into our everyday life. For a while, new mileage signs on the highways began to show both miles and kilometers, for example.

But President Reagan dismissed the Board in 1982, the idea being, let the rest of the world come around to our way of doing things. So we are in the distinguished company with two tiny third world countries in not being able to communicate with the rest of the world in this important area.

November 21: * The challenge of living with others is the greatest factor in brain development. Hence, the animals that live in packs or group communities have the best developed brains.

November 22: * About causality: "Everything causes everything else." Each event emerges out of an infinite web or network of causal relationships. Air resistance and friction can never be eliminated *in* *practice*; however, they can be eliminated in *thought experiments* and in the abstract world of mathematical physics. Causality, in physics, is therefore an idealization, a reality that exists only within the world of equations and computer simulations.

November 23: * This is about a fantastic human being: A Utah developer bought a lot of land along the Colorado River, put in a road, carved up the acreage into expensive lots, and built himself $600,000 mansion, hoping to stimulate interest in sales. The house sat directly across the road from a public camping area. After several years, when nobody came, a wealthy woman named Jennifer Speers bought the entire subdivision and had the mansion bulldozed! First she had everything that could be salvaged removed from the house. Now the land is in its original pristine state.

November 24: * In the part of the country where I was reared, and in the family I came from, faith was and is a deeply personal matter not to be cheapened by proselytizing or bumper stickers or loud public displays. It is too sacred for that. Prayer is offered in secret about what is on the mind and heart and then in silent meditation, we listen for answers. Within the stillness we can be attuned to the divine ideas or receive those ideas from others. We may feel reassurance or a boost of confidence when we need it most.

November 25: * Where there are hot climates, there are strong spices because in hot weather bugs grow, and spices kill them. In cold climates very bland food is served.

* From *Farmer-Stockman*, Nov. 2005: One in eight Mexican-born adults now lives in the United States.

November 26: * In 1870 or 1879, Manuel Nunes sailed from the island of Madiera, Portugal, to Hawaii aboard the Ravenscrag. He brought a musical instrument called a braguinho that the Hawaiians loved. They called it ukulele, which means "jumping flea." Manuel Nunes opened a shop and made the first ukulele for the Hawaiians. His grandson, Leslie Nunes, is said to have the largest collection of ukuleles in the world.

November 27: * William Butler Yeats, a special favorite, said, "Why should we honor those that die upon the field of battle [?], [A] man may show as reckless a courage in entering into the abyss of himself." It does take courage for self-examination, but I take exception to the first part. Fortunately for Yeats, he was never called upon to sacrifice on the battlefield. *Of course* we should honor those who die on the battlefield, boys (and girls) who probably never wanted to be there in the first place, and who were much too young to die.

Another group that is seldom called upon to make that sacrifice is generals. During the 2004 presidential campaign, General Wesley Clark, whom I (otherwise) admire, made the disparaging comment about Senator John Kerry (who earned a chestful of medals during the Vietnam War) that he, Clark was a general, whereas Kerry was a lieutenant. Kerry was asked for a reply, and he merely said, "A lot of lieutenants lost their lives in Vietnam." A lot of lieutenants lose their lives in any war—not as many as the enlisted men—but many more than generals. When is the last time you heard of a general losing his life in battle? And how much courage does it take for a Commander-in-Chief to declare war on another country? It isn't like the olden times, when generals led their troops into battle. If more people from the Pentagon, Oval Office and Congress were out in front of the troops, there probably wouldn't be as many wars.

November 28: * During this season when we celebrate our abundance, 59% of the people in the U.S. say religion plays a very important role in their lives as compared 31% of Britains, 30% of Canadians, 27% of Italians, 13% of Russians, 11% of Japanese, and 10% of French. (from *Pew Global Attitudes Project*)

In the last 15 years, credit card debt has gone from $210 billion to $985 billion. (*Statistical Abstract of the US*) Divorce rate per thousand: US: 6.2, as compared to Denmark, 4.0; Canada, 3.4; Japan, 3.1; Spain, 1.4; and Italy, 1.0. (*Monthly Labor Review*) Average yearly paid vacation days: Germany and Spain, 30; Britain, Australia, and Netherlands, 25; Japan, 18; China, 15, United States, 10. (*Bureau of Vital Statistics*)

November 29: * The Zapara people live in the Amazon forest. They are guided by their dreams, which is not all that different from what analytical psychologists do. In the 1970s anthropologists declared the Zapara extinct, but in fact there are 200 in Ecuador and about 150 in Peru. A hundred years ago, there were about 20,000 living along the banks of the Curaray, Conambo, Tigre, and Villano rivers. Then rubber companies came, and men and women of the tribe were made slaves and sold in the ports of Iquitos and Putumayo. Those who resisted were raped and killed. Rubber companies also brought sicknesses that killed off many of the natives. Then in 1941 a war between Ecuador and Peru divided the tribe between them. Then the Kichwa and Achuar invaded, killed the elders and settled in their territory. Then oil companies moved in. Now settlers are also coming.

Shamans are the political and spiritual leaders of the communities of Zapara. Gloria Ushigua, the daughter of a shaman, and a shaman and dreamer herself, last year traveled to New York for the third meeting of the UN Permanent Forum on Indigenous Issues. She said, "...we Zapara are are struggling for our future. It is dangerous because of the oil companies and settlers, but we are not afraid. What can we be afraid of? Disappearing? We know that we will disappear if we do not struggle. We want our lands to be demarcated and legalized...We have visited communities that are affected by the oil companies. The people are sick, the water is polluted, they are hungry because the animals and fish have gone away, and the children have disease on their skin. We are not ready."

November 30:* St. Andrew's Night, November 30, is the feast day of Scotland's patron saint, the first-century Galilean apostle, Andrew. The feast always includes the singing of "Auld Lang Syne," first published in the late 1600s, which was probably *not* originally written by Robert Burns. The feast includes haggis, bashed tatties and neeps.

* Roger Paulding provided this: According to the Alaska Department of Fish and Game, while both male and female reindeer grow antlers in the summer, male reindeer drop their antlers at the beginning of winter, usually late November to mid-December. Female reindeer retain their antlers till after they give birth in the spring.

So according to every rendition depicting Santa's reindeer, every single one of them, from Rudolph to Blitzen, had to be female.

December

December 1: * Theologian Martin Buber said, "We live in the currents of universal reciprocity." That seems like what Jesus said about, "Give and it shall be given to you," or what physicist David Bohm meant with his theory of Implicate Order, which says in effect that everything in the universe affects everything else because they're all part of the same unbroken whole. So the giver must also be the receiver. I can't give a blessing without receiving one in return. By giving time, talents, even positive thoughts, one receives inner peace.

Scottish researcher Kurt Hahn discovered while studying Royal Navy survival techniques during World War II that there are principles in human beings that drive them to help one another. This is probably in our primitive DNA. Bohm believes that when people are in situations that cause them to reach deep into themselves, they reach "the generating depth of consciousness which is common to the whole of mankind." Thousands of years ago our primitive forebears and the wilderness couldn't be separated. One was the context for the other, and vice versa. This harks again to the quantum theory about the inseparability of the observer and the observed.

* In dialogue, you're allowing the whole that exists to become manifest. "Seeing things whole" amounts to an inner shift in awareness and consciousness.

December 2: * If there is no trust and no receiving, there is no feminine principle operating.

* All mythology, from Japan to Mesoamerica, to ancient Greece, is a playing out of some variant of Mother Earth or Father Sky. The Earth Mother's is the great circle, birth-death-rebirth: the Eternal Return. Father Sky's is the quest, the journey from innocence to experience, from home to horizon, from dark to light.

* Pursuant to this, a man may impose the nurturing role on his wife, expecting her to mother him. He may be full of rage because his father didn't fulfill his fathering role, or he may carry a secret grief for his lost father. Sam Osherson, writing in *Finding Our Fathers*, says that only seventeen per cent of American men had a positive relationship with their fathers. The poet Robert Bly, who

has taken up the cause of reconnecting men with their feelings, says that, since the industrial revolution, the father-son relationship is the most damaged of all relationships. Each man carries a deep longing for his father and for his tribal fathers.

Jungian analyst Eugene Monick says in *Castration and Male Rage* that a primary enemy of men is fear of the feminine and fear of being wounded by other men. And Robert Moore and Douglas Gillette have written definitions in *King, Warrior, Magician, Lover: Rediscovering the Archetypes of the Mature Masculine* that are:

The king represents a man's power to take control, to make decisions. The shadow side of that, when the king feels his impotence, is virulent power, where he seeks control over others to compensate for his own deficits. His power lunches and big cars are actually symbols of powerlessness. (Poet W. H. Auden wrote: "Patriots? Little boys,/ obsessed by Bigness,/ Big Pricks, Big Money, Big Bangs.") The warrior represents the imperative that a man be prepared to fight for his integrity, for a cause or for justice. The shadow side of the warrior is the destroyer. The magician is the archetype of the shape-changer, the power of men to move mountains, to find a way to make things work. His shadow side is control, manipulation, sleight of hand and charlatanry. He is not to be trusted.

The lover walks between eros, the force for interconnection, and narcissism, the need for egoistic gratification.

December 3: * Antonio Gramsci spent a long period in fascist prisons, where he had no choice but to learn to live with himself. In a 1929 letter to his brother Carlo, he wrote that pessimism and optimism can arrive at creative synthesis only if one achieves "the profound conviction that...he has within himself the source of is own moral strengths, and that everything depends on him, on his energy, on his will." He ended his letter with a quote for French writer Romain Rolland: "I am a pessimist with my intelligence, but an optimist by my will."

Pessimism is the ruthless awareness of obstacles that truly exist. Optimism is faith in the possibility of facing obstacles while running the risk of defeat. The hero sees how things really are but doesn't allow her/himself to be checked by them. Nothing is beyond him and obstacles only cause him to become stronger.

December 4: * René Daumal says, "What is above knows what is below, but what is below does not know what is above....When one can no longer see, one can at least still know."

* Marguerite, Countess of Blessington: "Memory seldom fails when its office is to show us the tombs of our buried hopes."

December 5: * My cousin Jack's wife Ali Miller loves scones for breakfast. The word comes from the Gaelic word *sgonn*, meaning "shapeless mass." Both Jack and especially Ali are great cooks.

The Scots used "bread" to describe an oatcake or biscuit cooked on a bakestone or griddle. It becomes "shortbread" when you add shortening to the batter. Pinching around the edges of the shortbread comes from the ancient rites of sun worship. "Cake," as in "oatcake" comes from the Scots work *kaak*, meaning "slice."

In "better" parts of urban Scotland, residents are called "pan loafies" because they have an all-over crust, not just an upper crust.

December 6: * Things are not always what they seem. At this time of year we begin to sing, "O Come All Ye Faithful," one of my favorite carols. Actually, it was probably written by John Wade Frances as a coded rallying cry to all Jacobites. It was first heard just before the 1745 uprising.

December 7: * For anyone who is old enough, this date is indelibly etched in memory. It was the unthinkable: an attack on Americans at Pearl Harbor (although we didn't know exactly where that was), a strike that couldn't be ignored. It would mean war. I remember Daddy and Mother sitting close to the radio on that Sunday, or whenever it was that President Roosevelt spoke to the nation. Could have been Monday. The new baby was asleep. I was across the room, playing with my favorite doll and thinking that this was one more experience in my life. My exact thoughts (with a certain amount of anticipation) were: "I've never been in a war before."

December 8:* St. Francis of Assisi: "What you are looking for is what is looking."

* Thomas Merton: "In one sense we are always traveling, and traveling as if we did not know where we were going.

"In another sense we have already arrived.

"We cannot arrive at the perfect possession of God in this life, and that is why we are traveling and in darkness. But we already possess Him by grace, and therefore, in that sense, we have arrived and are dwelling in the light.

"But oh! How far have I to go to find You in Whom I have already arrived!" (from *Dialogues with Silence*)

* Also from Thomas Merton: "Solitude is not something you must hope for in the future. Rather, it is a deepening of the present, and unless you look for it in the present you will never find it." (from *The Sign of Jonas*)

December 9: * More evidence that no man is an island, and that we need each other for our own health. Historian Christopher Lasch wrote a book in 1979, *Culture of Narcissism,* in which he described the self-absorbed baby boomers, the "me generation," that critics blamed for everything from rising divorce and crime rates to child abuse and urban decay. Lasch said many Americans are so narcissistic that they can now perceive others only as a mirror of the self. Harvard Prof. Robert Putnam, in *Bowling Alone*, provides statistics showing a huge drop in all forms of public life since the 1960s and a corresponding rise in measures of malaise, from use of antidepressants to suicide rates. We also need each other for the health of our nation. As long ago as the 1830s, Alexis de Tocqueville warned that the tendency of Americans to do their own thing without regard for the needs of the larger group could doom our nation.

December 10: * My first piano teacher, Mrs. Virginia Manly Bryan, could produce miracles in me by her enthusiastic praise, and another teacher at West Texas Conservatory, Miss Ardath Johnson, who thought of herself as a concert pianist, could produce the opposite effect by her boredom. I remembered these lessons when I began teaching piano. Children blossom under praise and encouragement.

It works on adults, too. Especially during this busy season, I need to keep in mind the power of positive words that I can tell *myself*. I can recharge body and mind by remebering gentle, healing love. My mind and body do respond to my words. So I need to remember that love infuses every cell, muscle and organ with revitalizing energy, and healing is continually taking place, restoring my natural state of health. I am always in the presence of love. Because it is everywhere, I will discover it wherever I go, and I have more than enough time and energy to do what needs to be done.

December 11: * Headline in an Oregon paper: *Ill Gotten Gains: CEOs That Outsource Jobs Reward Themselves With Bigger Raises*

The story said that CEOs at companies that export the most jobs gave themselves bigger raises than their counterparts at companies that maintained more jobs in the U.S. That's the finding of a new study co-authored by United For a Fair Economy and the Institute for Policy Studies entitled "*Executive Excess 2004*." The compensation of CEOs at the 50 companies that outsourced the most service jobs rose 46% in 2003, compared to a 9% increase among CEOs at all 365 large companies surveyed by *Business Week*.

Another finding: If the minimum wage had increased as much as CEOs' pay since 1990, it would now be $15.76 per hour.

December 12: * Maybe the basis for Texans' unbounded confidence is the ancient geographical age of the state. It is the most stable land mass on the continent. But now that the societal structure is obviously crumbling, maybe earthquakes aren't far behind.

* The Economic Policy Institute's *The State of Working America 2004/2005,* found that workers are producing more but earning less. Worker productivity has been rising at an annual rate of 3.8% since 2000, compared to 2.4% increases in the high-growth 1990s. But the typical household has experienced a two-year drop of $1,300 in annual income when adjusted for cost-of-living increases.

December 13: * Nearly a third of the 275 largest and most profitable in the U.S. corporations paid little or no federal income taxes in 2001-2003, according to a study released in 2004 by Citizens for Tax Justice and the Institute for Taxation and Economic Policy.

Among the culprits were Verizon, AT&T and Boeing. Even some who did pay taxes paid very little: Intel paid federal taxes equaling just 15% of its corporate profits over the same three year period.

The data indicate that, in 2003, the average American taxpayer paid more federal income taxes than AT&T, Time Warner and Walt

Disney *combined!* Now does that turn your stomach?

December 14: * Faith is more than what I think is true. It is the substance out of which I form my belief. And my faith in love to heal, guide and prosper shapes what I experience. Like an acorn that holds the future mighty oak, faith is full with promise that there's even more of what love can accomplish through me and others than I can perceive or conceive. Faith is the assurance of things hoped for, the trust and belief in what is not yet seen. With this trust, I can accept healing, guidance, prosperity and comfort that are coming.

Things might actually be happening at the right time in the right way. Often what I perceive as chaos can also be looked at as just things rearranging themselves so that I can make a new beginning.

December 15: * It's devastating to be in the state of high flow and lose it. Creativity shuts down; all the synchronicity disappears. Then we need to step back and remember that we're operating in the flow of the universe. When we're on this wave-length, a natural sorting process is at work. The people who join us are, in their own way, moving along this same path. We care deeply for those with us, but we can't feel responsible for their success.

December 16: * When opening gifts, children don't hold back their excitement and joy. They accept their good and believe that they're worthy to receive it. Following their example, I accept the gift of life with joy and enthusiasm and a gratitude that nurtures my own health and well-being, because I know my life has value and meaning. Abundance comes in many forms and in many ways.

December 17: * Peru's very popular first woman Prime Minister Beatriz Moreno submitted her resignation after less than six weeks on the job because of media attacks concerning her sexual orientation. This is an outrage in light of the fact that the discovery of the so-called gay gene shows incontrovertively that sexual orientation isn't a choice. Color of skin isn't a choice, either, but if the media made the same attacks on the basis of race, people would call them bigots, unchristian. Ignorance in the uneducated isn't so bad, but ignorance of the media in a "civilized" country such as Peru is hard to believe.

The attacks must have been politically motivated, intended to play on the fears of the primitive thinker and the incredibly stupid.

December 18: * In 1980, Pope John Paul II ordered the Pontifical Academy of Science (an oxymoron that recalls George Bernard Shaw's observation that a Catholic university is a contradiction in terms) to review the case of Galileo Galilei, who, in 1633, was forced by the Italian Inquisition to retract his heretical teaching that the earth revolved around the sun. Eventually, after twelve years of deliberation, the Church conceded that Galileo was right. But as late as 1988, nothing had been done, and a Vatican official told a *Los Angeles Times* reporter, "The case is closed." Later, in ca. 1990, Joseph Ratzinger declared that the Church was correct to condemn Galileo's heliocentric views. Ratzinger is now Pope Benedict XVI. The Holy See has long thought it more important to ignore reality than admit a mistake.

December 19: * Amulets are ancient. Before we understood calamities and disease, they had immense power in people's lives. Amulets were sole defense against earthquakes, rivers changing course, babies dying. Amulets against gunfire are still believed in. The West Side Boys of Sierra Leone sport leather pockets containing *surah* from the Koran, just as the Sioux donned feathers and bells in defense against the white man's guns. An amulet's protection is magical rather than physical.

"Charm" and "talisman" are also protections. A charm brings good luck, health, and happiness and therefore protects against bad luck, sickness, and misery. A talisman, often used in ritual, is believed to have some magical property or power that can protect. But an amulet can also be an action, such as wearing a certain football jersey as protection against the other team.

The idea that a circle protects against invasion is behind many a necklace of amulets, as well as the neck torques that capture the soul, such as those of Thailand. Ankle bracelets protect African women from the underworld's evil spirits.

The protecting cirlce extends to Hinduism as well. In the *Ramayana*, Rama draws a circle around Sita and tells her to stay inside until he returns, to protect her from being stolen.

December 20:*According to traditional Irish lore, there is a plane of being somewhere between life and death called the "thin place," It is that place in time where the reality of this existence overlaps and intermingles with the reality of the existence beyond it.

* George Eliot: "Nothing is so good as it seems beforehand."

December 21: * This is my parents' wedding anniversary. James Hurley Miller and Ina Benson were married in 1926 and the union lasted almost 60 years. Nietzsche once observed that the primary purpose of marriage is conversation. The purpose of a committed relationship is not to take care of each other, to reinforce the parent-child complexes, but to grow through and with each other. Relationship is meant to be dialectical. From Psalm 133:1: "How very good and pleasant it is when kindred live together in unity."

Daddy depended on Mother and I think he never got over a sort of awe that she had married him. I doubt she ever fully realized that. Or maybe I'm wrong. At any rate, if she knew, she hid it well.

(In passing I might mention great disappointment when I learned that both Nietzsche and Aristotle were confirmed misogynists.)

December 22: * Irish comedians started out playing banjo. Comedian Eric Idle says the banjo is "the musical choice of the antisocial." Bill's artist buddy Chris Burkholder is a fantastic banjo player. His bluegrass is phenomenal! I wish there was somewhere for him to share his talent with the world.

December 23:* The Portuguese for "quince jelly" is *marmalade.* The Spanish for "jam" is *mermelada.* In the winter of 1700, a young Dundee grocer named James Keiller bought a whole shipment of Seville oranges, but he couldn't sell them because they were too bitter. So his wife used them instead of quinces, which were an ingredient in one of her old family recipes, and thus the famous marmalade was born

.

December 24: * We outgrow patterns, we outgrow people, we outgrow work. When we can't make the move forward, we fall back into an addictive pattern. Our ancestors developed skills that enabled them to survive. The hunter taught himself to concentrate on the target, aim, strike, bring home the hairy mastodon to the hungry clan. Centuries of patriarchal values still put the emphasis on goals, achievement, competition, production of consumables. Now we're beginning to reevaluate those values, because we're finding that life isn't worth living if we're always running as fast as we can after the mastodon. After all, how many mastodons can one cave hold?

December 25: * Marie-Louise Von Franz says, "It is the impulse of the divine to be incarnated." Christmas is about good tidings of great joy. Joy is a part of us that can never be separated from us because its source is the spirit of Love within.

Until as recently as the 1960s, Christmas wasn't a public holiday in Scotland. Offices and shops were open as usual until December 30, when the far more important holiday of Hogmanay was observed.

Until the year 1752, by our Gregorian calendar, people did not celebrate Christmas on this date, but on January 6, denoted as Christmas on the Julian calendar. Most people in Europe changed their calendars from Julian to Gregorian in 1582. Parts of Scotland moved the first day of its year from March 25 to January 1 in 1600. Russia switched in 1918.

When the Hindu god Krishna was born, long before Jesus, gifts brought to him were gold, frankincense, and myrrh.

December 26: * Boxing Day, when wealthy Britons boxed up their hand-me-downs to make room for their new gifts. These boxes were then presented to the servants. Boxing Day is still observed, but now the boxes contain new items.

* It's also time to think about how best to care for the beautiful Christmas plants. Poinsettias need daytime temperatures of 60-70 degrees (but not hotter) and can stand 55 degrees at night. The soil should be allowed to get completely dry before the plant is watered, and if the pot has foil around it, holes should be punched in the paper to allow water to drain off.

Christmas cactus, in this climate, can go outside in a protected place, like a porch, or after it has bloomed, it can be set in the garage (50 degrees). I seldom water it during its "dormant" stage. During a frost, it needs to come indoors. I set mine in a window and it decides when it wants to bloom again. One is too large to set in a window, but I've been told it likes to be root-bound, so I haven't tried to divide it into smaller pots. Prune after the blooms drop off.

Once Amaryllis bulbs have quit blooming, they can be set in a sunny window and watered and fed monthly until the leaves begin to yellow. Thereafter, water only sparingly and stop feeding. They need to be kept in their pots, even when put outside for warm weather. Bring them inside before frost-time and let them be dormant in a dark place until you see signs of new growth. Then water and fertilize and maybe add some new soil before placing them in a sunny spot.

December 27: * I do not face any challenge alone. But where would I be if not for grace—whatever it is? By grace, I am healed, prospered, loved, useful.

* Between 1876 and 1893 about seven million Texas cattle went through Doan's Crossing on the Red River, taking the Great Western Trail headed for Dodge City. That's about twice the number that moved up the Chisolm Trail.

Now, thanks to some Oklahomans, Dennis Vernon and John Barton, the enitre Great Western Trail is being marked, starting with Cameron County at Texas' tip, through Hidalgo, Brooks, Jim Wells, Live Oak, Atascosa, Bexar, Bandera, Kendall, Keff, Kimble, Menard, McCullough, Coleman, Callahan, Shakleford, Throckmorton, Baylor, Wilbarger Counties, with a marker put every six miles across 620 miles. To learn more about the Great Western Trail, contact Jeff Bearden (940) 552-4148.

I learned about this in *The Farmer-Stockman.*

* Poor timing: President Bush was already under fire for the longest summer vacation in presidential history, but he stayed on in Crawford as Katrina made landfall. Two days later, he took a photo op fly-over of the scene on the way back to Washington.

December 28: * Psychotherapist David Richo, author of *The Five Things We Cannot Change and the Happiness We Find by Embracing Them,* says the five things are:

1) Everything changes and ends.
2) Things do not always go according to plan.
3) Life is not always fair.
4) Pain is part of life.

5) People are not loving and loyal all the time.

December 29: * Trivia of a head: Scots King Malcolm III (Canmore; c. 1031-1093) married twice. His second wife was a Saxon princess, St. Margaret, probably born in Hungary while her father Edward was in exile. They had six sons and two daughters. (One was "good Queen Maud," who married Henry I of England.) Malcolm's ultimate resting place was Tynemouth, brought there in 1250, along with most of Margaret's remains. For unfathomable reasons, her head was taken by Mary, Queen of Scots, to Edinburgh Castle in 1560. Later it went to the Laird of Durie's house in 1567. The Jesuits took it in 1567, and from then it went to Antwerp in 1620, and to Scots College in Douai in 1627. Finally, during the French Revolution, St. Margaret's head disappeared completely.

December 30: * It is common practice in parts of the world to mark the year's end by a brief period of suspended animation, people behaving as if they were half-dead. In former times, fasting and other forms of austerity were practiced, and all activity ceased. This sort of year-end suspension can now be seen in Native American festivals ("the Fast"), Burma, Greece, and Mesoamerica, where five supplementary days (see below) were called "days without name," when all religious and civil business cease.

* December 30 is celebrated as Hogmanay in Scotland, and until the 1960s, it was much more important than Christmas. The name comes from the French *Hoguinané*. It is an Old Year's celebration, a time for haggis, bashed tatties and neeps, first footing, black bun (fruit cake), Het Pint, and skirling to bagpipes. In olden times the doors were left open to allow the spirit of the Auld Year to slip away. Hogmanay has been celebrated for over 200 years in Kirkwall, Orkney Islands, with ball games for both men and boys starting with a ball thrown down from the Mercat Cross.

December 31: * With the inaccuracies of early calendars, extra days were often added at the end of the year to square the lunar and solar cycles. This practice is the origin of the so-called Twelve Days of Christmas. In Scotland the Twelve Days of Christmas are called solar cycles. This practice is the origin of the so-called Twelve Days of Christmas. In Scotland the Twelve Days of Christmas are called "Daft Days." During this period from Christmas to January 6, at Oxford and Cambridge the Lord of Misrule reigned.

* On this day in 1946, President Truman officially proclaimed the end of World War II, and we all believed that a brighter America was ahead. For a decade, we were right.

* And now, in the words of Rainer Marie Rilke, "...let us welcome the new year, full of things that have never been."

Index

C

D

N

O

P